GCSE music course notes

John Montgomery and Peter Kay

Includes 34 track CD

CD produced by Andrew Montgomery

with special thanks to Brian Carty, Sheila Cochrane, Bob Dewar, Emily Dewhurst, Rosemary Macrae, Carolynn McIntyre, Carol McMillan, Kathryn McPhee, Bruce Ryan and John Stephenson

Leckie & Leckie

GCSE Music Course Notes © Copyright John Montgomery and Peter Kay 2001

GCSE Music CD © copyright Leckie & Leckie 2001. All compositions licensed with permission from the copyright holders. All compositions and arrangements © John Montgomery except *Jeux d'Adresse* © Peter Kay, *Bangla Dhun* © Harrisongs Ltd, *Sab Vird Karo Allah Allah* © Oriental Star Agencies, *Gending Langiang* © EMI, *Un Aeroplano a Vela* © Label Bleu, *Fato Consumado* © Som Liver, *La Bamba* © Koka Media Ltd, *Jump For Joy* © Rituals Music Ltd, *Trinidad Farewell* © Phonographic Performance Ltd, *Dance of the Women* © Delta Music, *Serengetti* © De Wolfe Publishing Ltd, *Rokudan* © Delta Music, *The Hallelujah Chorus* © Polygram, *O Mio Babbino Caro* © Silva Screen, *Prélude à l'après-midi d'un faune* © Polygram, *The Rite of Spring* © Polygram, *Classical Symphony No. 1* © Polygram, *Music for Strings, Percussion and Celeste* © Polygram, *Horn Concerto No. 4* © Polygram, *Violin Concerto in D Major* © Polygram, *Mars - from The Planets Suite* © ABM Music Ltd, *A Life on the Ocean Wave* © Grasmere, *Tritsch-Tratsch Polka* © Grasmere, *I Want to Talk About You* © Charly. With thanks to the people at all the above companies who made this possible.

All rights reserved. Copying prohibited. No part of this publication may be reproduced, stored in a retrieval system, or transmitted in any form or by any means, electronic, mechanical, photocopying, recording or otherwise, without prior permission in writing from Leckie & Leckie. Legal action will be taken by Leckie & Leckie against any infringement of our copyright.

Published by
Leckie & Leckie
8 Whitehill Terrace
St Andrews
United Kingdom KY16 8RN
tel: 01334 475656
fax: 01334 477392
hq@leckieandleckie.co.uk
www.leckieandleckie.co.uk

ISBN 1-898890-08-0

A CIP Catalogue record for this publication is available from the British Library.

Printed in the UK by Inglis Allen, Kirkcaldy on environmentally friendly paper. The paper is made from a mixture of sawmill waste, forest thinnings and wood from sustainable forests.

® Leckie & Leckie is a registered trademark.

Leckie & Leckie Ltd is an Investor in People company.

John Montgomery was Head of Music at Preston Lodge High School for fifteen years before becoming a freelance writer and composer. He has had several books published in the field of music education. His musicals *Once Upon A Castle* and *Deacon Brodie* are widely performed, and Leckie & Leckie are about to publish his new group performance pack *Young Jazz*.

Peter Kay taught music in secondary schools in South Yorkshire for sixteen years, the last nine of which he was Head of Music at Adwick School, Doncaster. He is currently programme leader for music education courses at the University of Sunderland. He also works as a GCSE Music Moderator.

CONTENTS

INTRODUCTION · 6
About the Course · 6
This Book and CD · 6
Assessment · 6

PERFORMING · 7
Solo Performing · 8
Ensemble Performing · 10

COMPOSING · 11
Introduction · 12
1. Pentatonic · 15
2. Blues · 20
3. Developing Ideas – Part-writing · 25
4. Ostinato · 31
5. Improvise · 35
6. Words · 42
Writing it Down · 50

LISTENING AND APPRAISING · 57
Introduction · 58
Table of Composers · 59
World Music · 60
Ragtime – Concepts at Work · 66
The Voice · 70
Music of the 20th Century · 75
Shape and Form · 78
Instrument File · 81

GLOSSARY OF CONCEPTS · 84

LIST OF CD TRACKS · 91

INTRODUCTION

About the Course

GCSE Music is a two-year course in which you will study three interrelated areas:

- **Performing (Solo and Ensemble)**
- **Composing**
- **Listening and Appraising**

This Book and CD

This book and CD are about these three areas. They will help you both in the classroom and at home in understanding what is required to complete the course successfully.

The book is divided into Performing, Composing, and Listening and Appraising sections. Key concepts you should know are highlighted **in blue** throughout the text. You will also find concise definitions of these concepts in the Glossary on pages 84 to 90.

The CD is designed to be used as you work through the book. It has ideas for composing and extracts of varying styles of music. A list of the 34 tracks on the CD is given on pages 91 and 92.

Assessment

You will be awarded an overall grade based on a combination of all your marks.

Solo Performing is assessed by your teacher. You will play a piece on your solo instrument. The performance will be recorded and the results checked by an external moderator.

Ensemble Performance is also assessed by your teacher. You will perform a piece in a group of usually up to five players but this is negotiated with your teacher. The assessments made by your teacher will be checked by an external moderator.

Composing is assessed mainly by your teacher but there may also be an externally set composition task. An external moderator will check the assessments made by your teacher.

Listening and Appraising are things we do all the time as musicians and they will be assessed in an exam at the end of your course. The listening exam may focus on specific areas of study on which you have been concentrating throughout the course. It is mainly short answers with some multiple-choice questions.

PERFORMING

PERFORMING

Solo Performing

During your GCSE course you will play contrasting styles of music in preparation for this part of the assessment.

What you are aiming for

At various points during or at the end of the course you will be asked to perform on your main instrument. This performance will be recorded and assessed. The standard of piece you play and how well you play will determine the mark you are eventually awarded. You may also have the opportunity to perform on a second instrument.

Performing with confidence

This is easier said than done! However, there are steps you can take to help control those nerves. The most obvious one is *be prepared*.

It is good to be a bit nervous. Most good performers feel butterflies in the stomach. You will think more quickly and react more swiftly but the difficult bit is keeping it all under control!

Points to remember

1. **Get into the routine of regular practice – this will pay off at exam time. Not doing enough during the course and then having a great flurry of activity just before the big day doesn't work.**

2. **Try to record your pieces. This is very important as it not only gives you an accurate record of your work, but it also gives you the opportunity to listen to yourself. We are often too busy playing a piece to listen carefully. You'll be amazed at the things you'll hear. This is often a very good way of finding and correcting mistakes, e.g. unexplained changes in speed!**

3. **Practise playing your pieces to your friends and relatives – this will give you confidence – and your audience will (hopefully) enjoy it!**

4. **When you go into the exam, remind yourself how hard you have worked over the last couple of years. Relax, and decide that the examiner is going to enjoy your performance. A smile and a 'hello' will help put you at your ease.**

5. **Take your time and make sure you are happy with the set up: for example, can you see the accompanist? Check the examiner can see you clearly. Sort out these matters with your teacher before the exam to increase your confidence and improve your performance.**

6. During your exam you may make a few small mistakes. Do not worry if this happens. Every performer makes mistakes no matter how good they are. Though your playing has to be accurate in every way, your mark will be based on your overall interpretation of the music (how well you have expressed the music).

7. Although you will be a bit nervous, remember that the examiner wants you to do your best, and knows how you will be feeling. Your examiner is also your music teacher and he/she will put you at your ease. Remember that he/she will be trying to pass you and give you the best possible result.

8. If you are playing an electronic keyboard (or other instrument which has settings), make sure you are organised in advance and that you are completely familiar with its settings and operations.

9. If your exam is in the morning, get up early – especially if you are singing or blowing!

Review Details
SOLO PERFORMING
- Perform one solo piece
- Assessed by your teacher but externally moderated
- Practise regularly throughout the course
- Perform regularly in front of family and friends
- Record your practice pieces at home and/or school
- On the day, be there in plenty of time
- Be sure you know the set-up arrangements inside the performance room
- Relax and enjoy the performance

Ensemble Performing

Playing in an ensemble is a very important and enjoyable part of music-making. Remember, performing with your instrument or voice in an ensemble is just as important as performing your solo piece. During your course you will have opportunities to play in different instrumental and vocal ensembles.

You will be assessed on how well you can perform with your instrument or voice and how well your playing fits in with other musicians. You will be assessed and recorded during or at the end of the course.

Points to remember

1. An 'ensemble' can be as few as two performers. Generally, there should be no more than five performers, but you may be able to negotiate this with your teacher. Not all members of the ensemble have to be part of your music group.

2. Extra rehearsal time may be needed. Difficulties with instruments or music may occur. It is important that you are sensitive and helpful to the needs of others in your ensemble. Carefully plan the way you use your rehearsal time.

3. When the time comes to record and assess your performance it is very important that your part can be heard clearly. No one else should be playing the same part as you. It's up to you to make sure that your ensemble works well together.

4. You need to have copies of the music you are performing wherever possible.

Review Details
ENSEMBLE PERFORMING
- Assessed by your teacher, marks checked by external moderator
- Make sure your part can be heard clearly on the tape
- Try to have music copies of the piece wherever possible
- As in solo work, regular practice is essential
- Be considerate and help other members in the ensemble
- Plan your time carefully

COMPOSING

COMPOSING

Introduction

One of the most exciting areas of GCSE Music is the Composing element. The two activities in this element are:

- **Composing**
- **Improvising**

These both mean creating something new, something which is new to you – the composer.

Composing means creating a completely new piece of music (e.g. a song, a piece for a group of instruments, or a soundscape).

Improvising means making up music spontaneously ('on the spot'). The most common way to improvise is to create melody over a given set of chords.

During your course you will build up a folio of compositions. You should record these on cassette or disc. At the end of the course your teacher and you will choose the compositions which represent your best work. These will form the coursework part of the assessment which your teacher will mark. This mark will be moderated externally.

You may also be asked to compose a particular type of music towards the end of the course. You will learn how to work in different structures and frameworks. All you will have to do is apply what you have learned to the task set.

What's composing all about?

Think of composing music as something which is *natural* for us all to do – because it is! When someone asks you to draw a face for example, you do not consider whether you can or not – you can. You are asked to give this face a large nose and tiny eyes, and a pimple on the cheek – no problem. Now you are given a big paint box and brush. Give your face a black moustache, bright red lips and a blue hat. Wrap a long striped scarf around the neck. You've done exactly as you were asked. Is it good? Well, maybe. It might be better next time you try.

Someone else asks you to write down exactly what happened in your life yesterday: all the details of where you went, who you spoke to, what time you went to bed, etc. Now you are asked to change some of these details. Invent a place you would have liked to have gone to. What amazing person did you meet? You landed up in a yellow taxi in New York – it's snowing hard – a man with a gun breaks into your taxi as you stop at the lights on Fifth Avenue. All you can remember is that he has a moustache and is wearing a long striped scarf! How good is your story? Maybe great and maybe not. However, you have created it. It has shape and direction: it starts, it ends and so on.

Creating music is just like this, whether it be improvising or composing. You are going to say something new and refreshing and you don't have to be Beethoven or The Beatles.

You may already be a budding young composer – or this may be your first attempt. Whatever, everyone can create something new. Don't panic – the ideas will come.

Once you have learned how to create ideas and place them within a simple structure, you can explore and enjoy your composing – as well as receiving a good final result for your trouble!

The starting point

A stimulus is the starting point of a composition: it is 'the spur', 'the spark', 'the first idea'.

Here are some examples of a stimulus:

A poem about a train journey What instruments could represent the rhythm of the train? What scenes go by the train window? How could you describe them in sound? Would the piece start slowly? How would you construct your music? How would you represent the power of the train?

The inside of a large clock Each part moves and repeats perfectly. With all of these moving parts, would you want to have several different types of sounds or instruments playing? Would each instrument play the same pattern of notes over and over?

Film of a new space exploration What effects could you use to represent the spacecraft? How do you time your music accurately with a given video sequence? Did something go terribly wrong on this mission? Would long sustained sounds or short staccato notes represent the flight into space?

A seascape You have chosen a chord progression to improvise over. What effect could you use to represent the gentle swell of the ocean? Trills, with gradual changes in volume? Long notes to represent the calm? Staccato notes with chromatic runs as the weather changes?

These are a few suggestions you may wish to return to and use as a stimulus for a future composition. There are endless other stimuli. Always ask yourself questions when you have decided on an idea: what form will my piece take; what instruments are available to me and who is going to play them; what effect do I want to create?

The answers to these questions will probably change during the course of your composing. Don't worry! It's a healthy sign that your ideas and thoughts are evolving, changing and progressing.

Six composing frameworks

It is essential to use a framework (a structure) around which to create your musical compositions. Here are six different frameworks for composing music with examples of each on the CD:

1. **Pentatonic**
2. **Blues**
3. **Developing Ideas – Part-writing**
4. **Ostinato**
5. **Improvise**
6. **Words**

1. Pentatonic

The **pentatonic scale**, or five-note scale, has been in existence for many centuries. Civilisations from China to Africa and India to Ireland have based melodies upon it. Unlike the **major** and **minor** scales, the pentatonic scale usually has no **semitones**.

The pentatonic scale has been used to create compositions all over the world. Elements within these compositions (such as rhythm, harmony, tempo and instruments used) help us to recognise where the compositions come from.

For instance, if you wanted to create a Japanese-sounding melody, you would have to think carefully about what type of instrumental sound you would use: possibly a harp-like plucking sound or a haunting whistle where you might slide or bend the notes to create a Far-Eastern effect. You may discover these sounds on a guitar, a keyboard or a recorder. Experiment with several different instruments and objects – you'll be amazed at the unlikely sources you will find for the effect you want to create. Or maybe you want to write a melody with a convincing Scottish flavour. Will it be a fast-moving **jig** with triplets, or a slow **waltz**? You may wish to include **Scotch snaps** as part of your rhythm pattern.

If you have access to a keyboard, play the five different black notes **ascending** and **descending**. This is a pentatonic scale no matter which note you start on. Now try playing them in any order to make a simple tune. No matter which order, with some simple rhythm you should end up with a pleasing melody.

To keep things simple, let's make our first note G as in the diagram below and call it note 1.

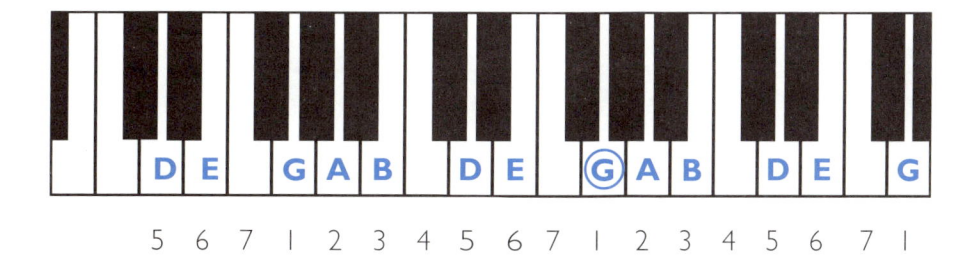

D	E	G	A	B	D	E	G	A	B	D	E	G
5	6	7	1	2	3	4	5	6	7	1	2	3	4	5	6	7	1

Now you are going to add notes 2, 3, 5 and 6 to make a pentatonic scale.

You can also use the same notes in a different **octave** above or below, to add interest as in the diagram above.

Phrases

When you create a melody, try to think of it in phrases just as words are grouped together, for example:

Question: 'How are you today?'
Answer: 'I'm very well, thank you.'

Groups of notes make a phrase (a statement), and, as in the spoken or written word, there is often a question/answer relationship between the phrases. Here are two examples of question and answer musical phrases:

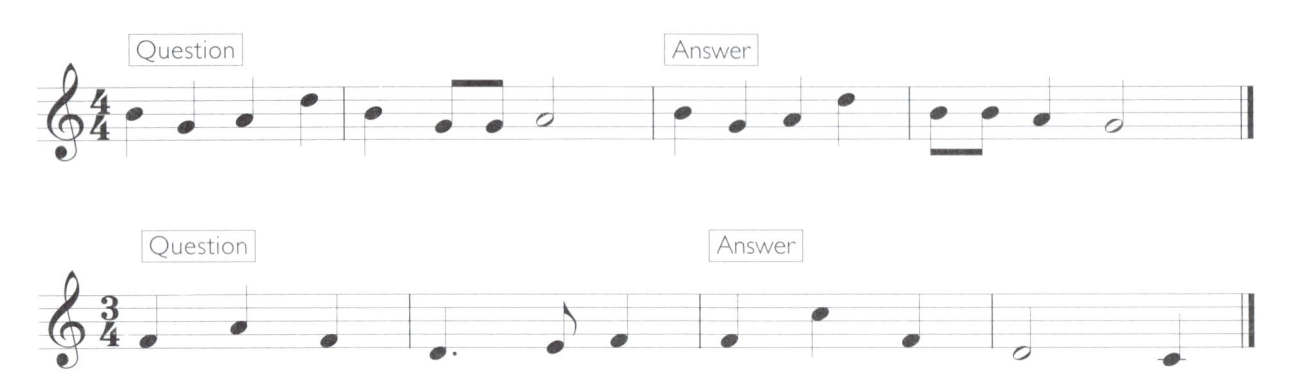

Think too about the *shape* of your melody. How many bars will it have and how many beats will be in each bar? It is common to have eight or sixteen bars to give you a simple and balanced structure.

Each of your phrases could be made up of two bars: two bars for the question and two bars for the answer. Repeating phrases help to strengthen the melody and give it continuity.

Accompanying your melody

Once you have created the phrases, try accompanying your pentatonic melody with simple chords.

Use chords on the keyboard, guitar or piano or have a friend play along with you. Start your melody on a G, a B or a D and make your first chord G. Using the notes G, A, B, D and E try to fit in the following chords as an accompaniment:

Chord of G

Chord of C

Chord of D

You will soon hear that the notes G, B and D in the melody 'fit' the chord of G. Now see which notes fit the chord of C, remembering to avoid using the *note* C in your melody.

Start your piece with the chord of G, and experiment using the chords of C and D against the pentatonic melody you have created. Finish your piece using the chord of G.

Record your piece on tape and write down its note names. For help with writing your piece down using notation, turn to *Writing it Down* on page 50.

Here is an example of a pentatonic melody. See if you can play it and compare it with your own composition. Notice that it follows the pattern of 'question and answer' phrases.

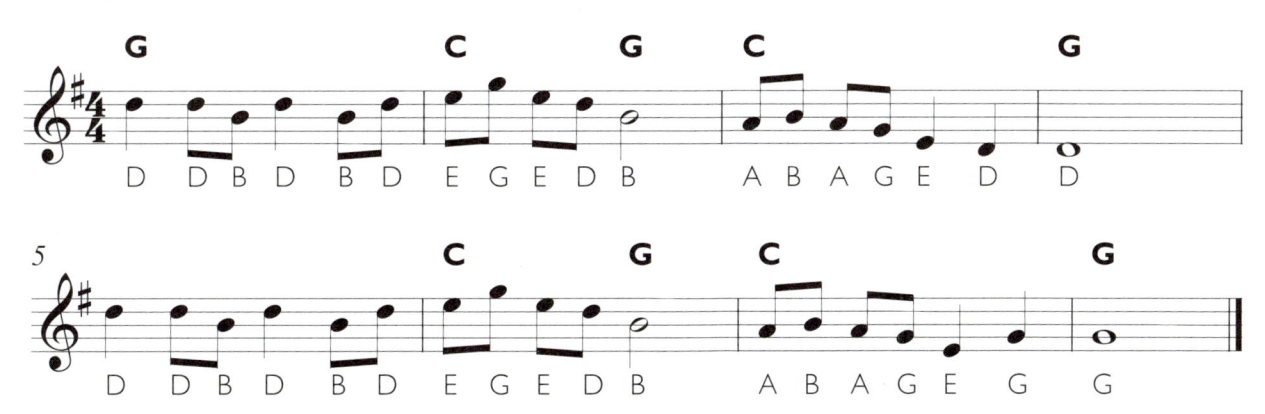

[Musical notation: Pentatonic melody in G major, 4/4 time]

Line 1 (bars 1-4):
- G: D D B D | C: B D E G E D B | G: A B A G E D | C: D (half note), G: D (whole note)

Line 2 (bars 5-8):
- D D B D | C: B D E G E D B | G: A B A G E | C: G, G: G

The notes of G, A, B, D and E have been used in this pentatonic tune, suggesting the key of G. We have also used the chords I, IV and V (in this case G, C and D). The chords I, IV and V are called primary chords. They are the most common combination of chords used for accompaniment in all music, no matter what the style, and they are often called the 'three-chord trick'.

Because we are in the key of G, we have made G the first chord of the piece.

Rhythm

To suggest a particular 'feel' in your composition you could introduce a 'thumbprint' (a feature) which will make your piece more convincing. *Japanese Garden* (CD track 1) uses alternate crotchets and quavers based around repetition of the note D. We could call this the piece's 'thumbprint' or 'signature'.

Use *similar* rhythms throughout your piece to make it sound continuous and connected.

Try to complete your piece in the key of G adding chords to it. Record your piece and try to write it down.

Extension work

Now we are going to extend our melody and give it a middle section. We are also going to add two new chords – the chord VI and the chord II. These are minor chords commonly used to add interest and to take us away briefly from our other three chords.

Because *Japanese Garden* is in the key of G, the new chord VI will be E minor which contains the notes E, G and B. The chord II will be A minor containing the notes A, C and E. So already you can see that these are notes you could use in your melody against these chords.

You will see that the piece has a definite form: it is in three distinct sections, called ABA. This a very common shape for music to be in. This ABA layout is called **ternary form**. 'A' is the first section; 'B' is a new or different section; 'A' is a repeat of the first section.

Here is the complete piece called *Japanese Garden* in the key of G. Listen to the piece on your CD and then play it on the keyboard or on the instrument of your choice.

CD1 Japanese Garden

What You Should Know

- **Major and minor scales** are the two types of scales used in most Western music
- **Semitones** – the distance of a half tone between notes
- **Jig** – a quick Irish or Scottish dance
- **Waltz** – a dance of moderate speed, with three beats to the bar
- **Scotch snaps** – two notes of which the first one is played quickly, on the beat
- **Pentatonic scale** – has five notes and does not usually use semitones
- **Octave** – the distance between one note name and the next same note name
- **Ascending notes** – notes becoming higher in pitch
- **Descending notes** – notes becoming lower in pitch
- **Ternary Form** – a piece of music in three parts, the first and third being the same

JAPANESE GARDEN
melody

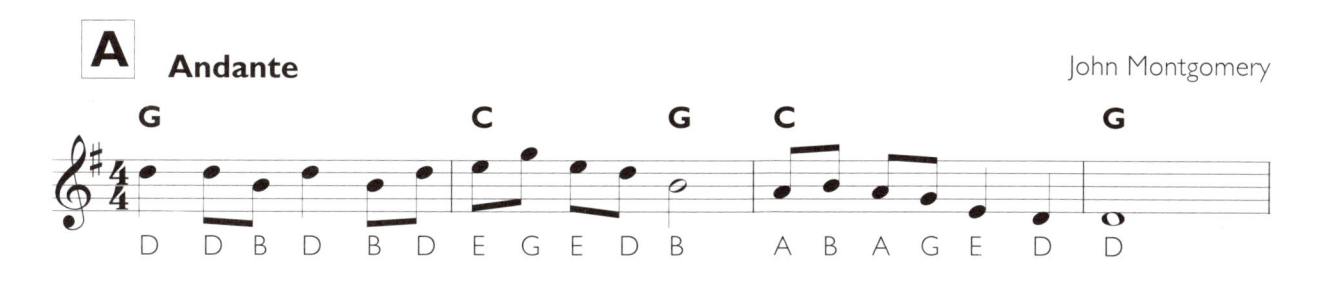

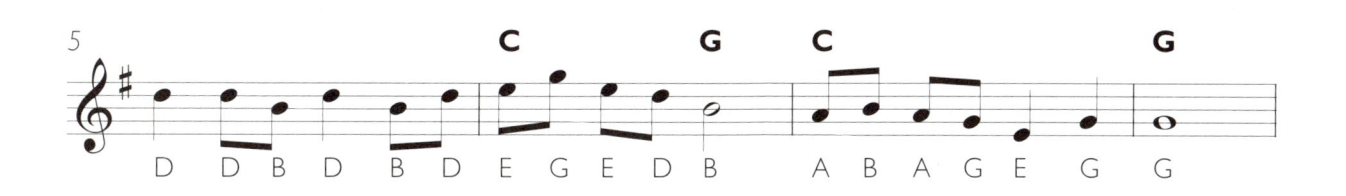

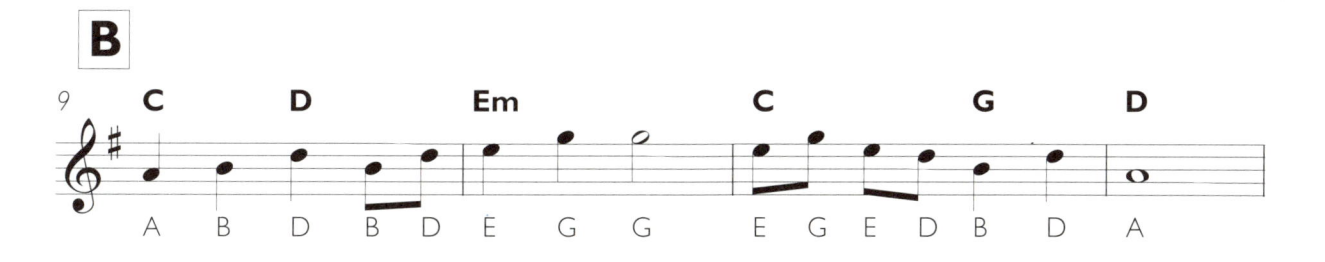

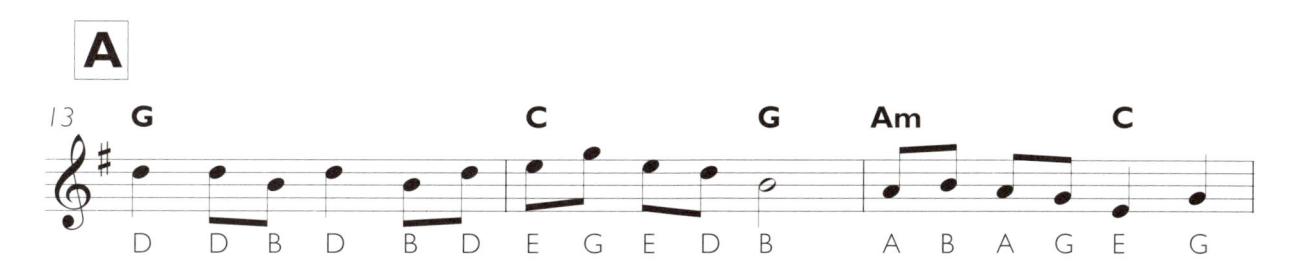

A Andante

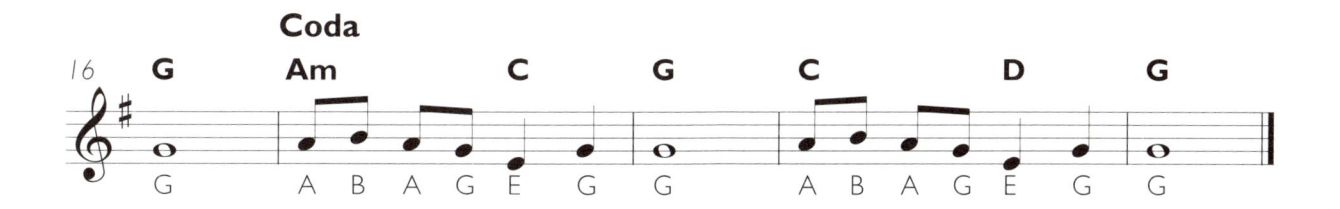

John Montgomery

2. Blues

Blues is an early and very important form of jazz. This style of music has its roots in the terrible misery which black people endured in the 18th and 19th centuries when millions of them were brought from Africa to the USA and sold as slaves. Conditions were very poor and families were often broken up. Most were sent to work in the cotton fields of the southern states of Louisiana, Alabama and Georgia. To express their hardship and their hopes for the future they sang spirituals. These songs were originally lines from the Bible, but through time and improvisation their meanings altered.

When black people started to move to the big industrial cities, such as Chicago and St Louis, after slavery was abolished in 1865, the Blues became popular throughout the USA. Blues are slow jazz songs often relating to blacks' continuing struggle for equality and basic living and working conditions.

Blue notes

Using the key of C, here are the notes which make up the Blues scale. The notes of Eb and Bb are called **blue** notes. Another blue note often used is F#. Using blue notes gives the music a feel of both major and minor.

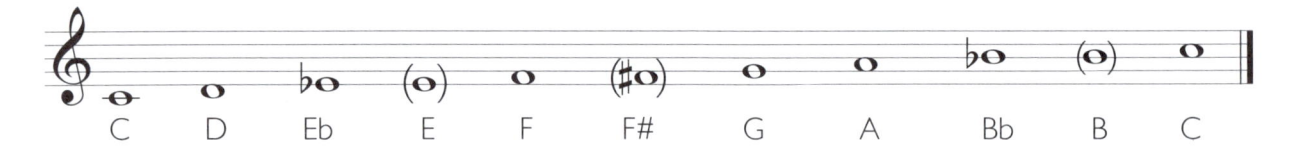

C   D   Eb   E   F   F#   G   A   Bb   B   C

Blues Scale (the notes in brackets can also be used)

Blues songs and tunes often use **syncopation** and dotted rhythms in their melody, while the accompaniment remains very straightforward. Try to clap this rhythm. It appears in the Blues song *Carolina Blues* on the CD.

The Twelve-Bar Blues

Blues songs use a particular scale and a simple framework of chords, called the twelve-bar blues.

In the key of C, the **chords** which typically make up a twelve-bar blues are:

C / / / C / / / C / / / C / / /

F / / / F / / / C / / / C / / /

G / / / F / / / C / / / C / / /

Below are slight variations which you could try out:

C / / / F7 / / / C / / / C7 / / /

F / / / F / / / C / / / C / / /

G / / / F7 / / / C / / / C / / /
                   (or G7 when repeating verse)

Using the formula that in the key of C, C = chord I , F = chord IV, and G = chord V you can now change this to any key which suits you.

Using the twelve-bar blues is an exciting way to create a new composition, arrangement or improvisation.

How to start your Blues piece

Line 1. C / / / F / / / C / / / C / / /

Use slow single finger chords or piano/guitar chords as a backing, and try to sing or play a line using the notes of the Blues scale. Make the last note of your melody line longer. It may help you to sing some words along to your melody.

Line 2. F / / / F / / / C / / / C / / /

Use the same melody as for line 1. Don't worry if it doesn't sound good yet. This is the time for trial and error and for experimenting.

Line 3. G / / / F / / / C / / / C / / /

For this line you may want to introduce some new notes that will work with the chord of G. Reintroduce a few notes from your first line to round the melody off. Make sure your last melody note is longer, to make the verse sound complete.

Check again with the Blues scale, especially the blue notes. Have you included any? Write your composition down in any way and worry about the details later. Your teacher will offer you good tips and advice and show you short cuts for putting your ideas down on paper.

Now that you have put a verse or tune together over the given chords, think about an introduction. An introduction sets the speed and mood of the music. An easy introduction is one bar of C chord and one bar of G7 chord.

One other device often used is adding a verse of instrumental melody only. This is called an instrumental or instrumental break and is often an improvisation based on the melody.

Here is the first line of *Carolina Blues*:

See how we have used the blue note Eb against the chord of C. That same note will work well against the F chord in line 2 when the phrase is repeated.

Here are the melody and chords for *Carolina Blues*. Play the music and see how the notes in line 3 complete the verse. The notation is an approximate guide to the CD vocal recording.

CAROLINA BLUES

Blues Swing 88

John Montgomery

(Goin' to Car - o - li - na — back to where my girl should
be I'm goin' to Car - o - li - na — back to where my girl should
be And I know if I don't find her
Lord it will be the end of me My)

(heart's in Car - o - li - na that's what I tell the Lord a -
bove My heart's in Car - o - li - na that's what I tell the Lord a -
bove Got to get back to my wo - man
'cause she's the on - ly one I love)

CD2 Carolina Blues

Now try putting together your own Blues tune or song. You may find it helpful to write your piece in a different key from *Carolina Blues*. Here are the twelve-bar blues chords and blues scales for the keys of G and D.

Twelve-Bar Blues Chords in G

G / / / G / / / G / / / G / / /

C / / / C / / / G / / / G / / /

D / / / C / / / G / / / G / / /

(D7 / / / if repeating)

COMPOSING

23

Blues Scale in G

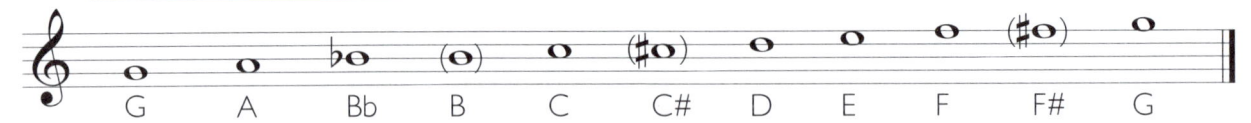

G A Bb B C C# D E F F# G

(notes in brackets are optional)

Twelve-Bar Blues Chords in D

D / / / D / / / D / / / D / / /

G / / / G / / / D / / / D / / /

A / / / G / / / D / / / D / / /

(A7 / / / if repeating)

Blues Scale in D

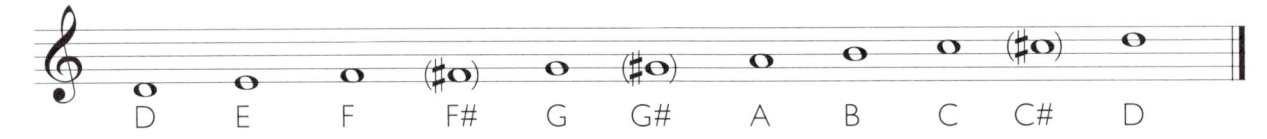

D E F F# G G# A B C C# D

(notes in brackets are optional)

What You Should Know

- **Blues** – slow early jazz songs, about hardship but not usually religious
- **Improvising** – making up (creating) music on the spot, over given chords
- **Twelve-bar blues** – a common framework of three chords to accompany blues
- **Blue notes** – notes introduced into a scale to give it a 'bluesy feel'
- **Syncopation** – accenting notes on the 'weak' beats, or off the beat, 'pushed'

3. Developing Ideas – Part-writing

Composing does not stop at having ideas and writing them down or recording them. The next step is to use your ideas to create an interesting piece of music. You have to decide when your composition can be developed more and when it is finished. There are many ways of developing and extending your ideas – here are just a few:

Part-writing

If you have decided to compose a melody which you would like to be performed by instruments or voices then you can use the following method of extending it. Once you have composed a melody, decided what key it is in (your teacher will help you here) and added chords to it, you can make it much more interesting if you arrange it for more than one instrument or voice.

Take this simple melody:

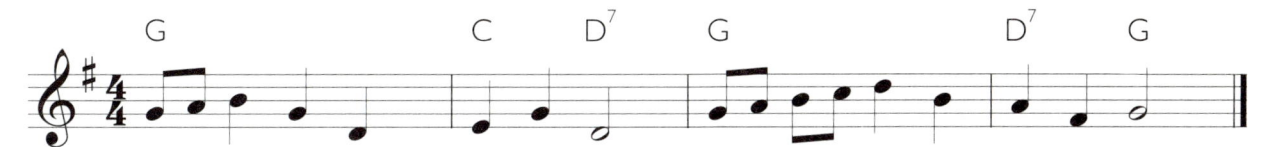

We now add parts to it in steps. First of all, we could add a very simple second part using the roots (name notes) of the chosen chords:

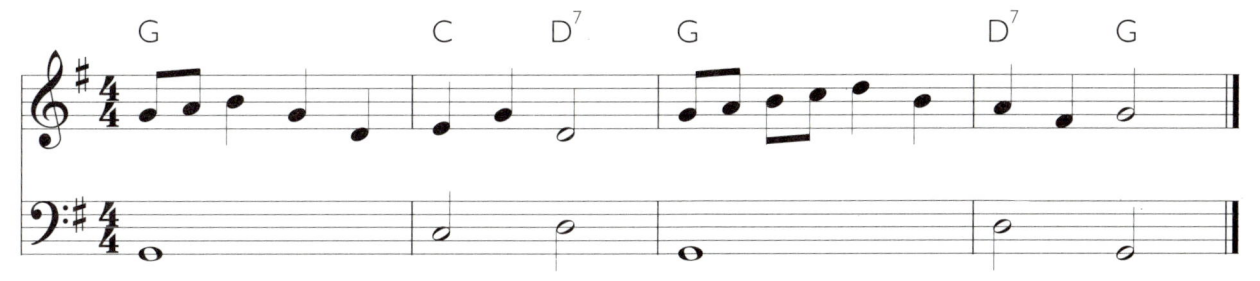

Notice that the second part is written in the bass clef – it is often better to write a lower part as your second part. If you are going to write your composition out, study the *Writing it Down* section on pages 50 to 56.

Now play the melody and the second part together. You may wish to use a sequencer or ask a friend to help you if you cannot play both parts at once. Next, decide if you like the sound of any of the other notes of the chosen chords in the bass line instead of the roots. Always play your music through several times – remember that it's how it sounds to you, the composer, that really matters.

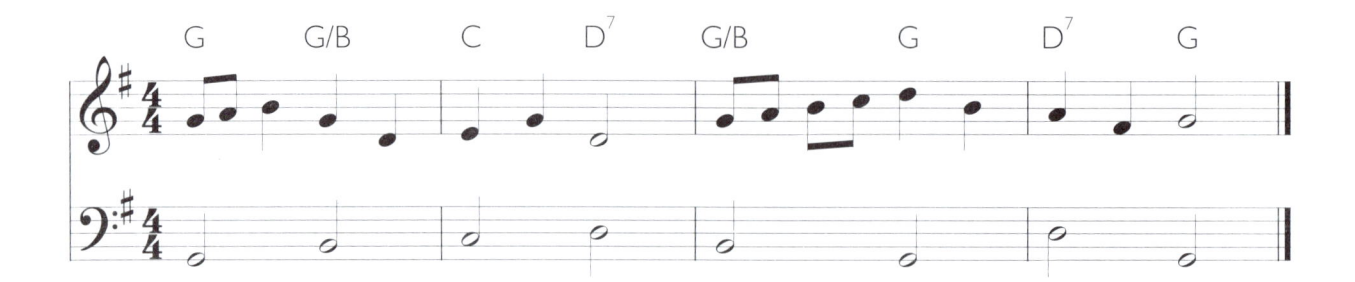

Notice that most of the notes chosen here are either the root (name note) or the third of the chord (second note up in the chord). This is quite common.

Now experiment with your bass line to see if you can put any extra notes in to make it sound more interesting. These extra notes usually move by steps. There may even be sections where your second part can copy your original melody. This is called **imitation** – look at bar 3 below, for example:

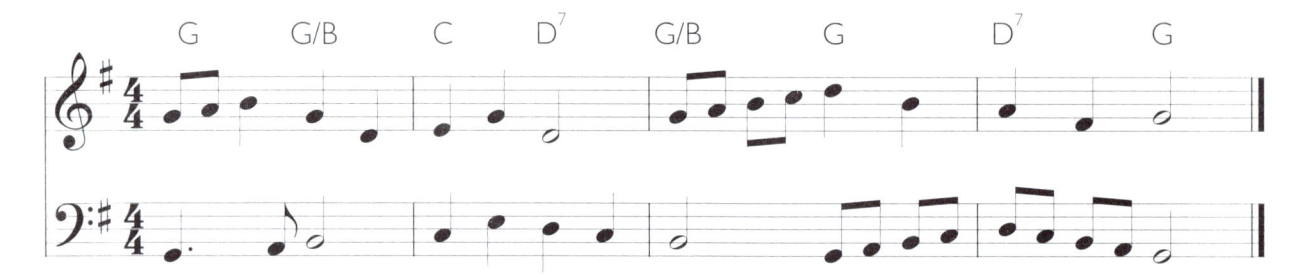

When adding a second part, it is a good idea to try to make it move in the opposite direction to the first part, i.e. when the first part moves downwards, the second part moves upwards. This is called **contrary motion**. It isn't always possible, but you should try to arrange your parts this way if you can.

Once you have composed a second part you may wish to add a third and even a fourth part. You would use the same process, but remember that if you have too much going on in the music your ideas will not be clear. It is a good idea to use rests (silences). Play your composition to yourself – you should always be able to hear your original tune, but it doesn't always have to be in the top part!

Study the example at the top of page 27 to see how a third part could be included. (Notice that the beginning of the second bar of the second part is very similar to the beginning of the first bar of the first part – except it has been turned upside down – this is called **inversion**.)

Some melodies are not in keys – these are known as **atonal** melodies. Playing these melodies over and over to yourself and really listening to them is even more important here. You cannot rely on the chords being the 'usual' ones. Instead, you have to select the sounds which you like.

Extending a melody

There are many ways of extending a melody. The easiest way is simply to repeat a section. We use this method in composition, often as a way of organising the music into some kind of form or structure. You can read more about this in the *Shape and Form* section on pages 78 to 80. However, sometimes we simply repeat something because we think it sounds good and want to hear it again.

More often, we repeat things with modifications. One of the main ways of doing this is to use a device called **sequence**. This is when we repeat part of a tune or phrase at a higher or lower pitch. Most of the major composers, from Bach to Lloyd-Webber have used this method. For example, this simple melody:

can be extended using a sequence like this:

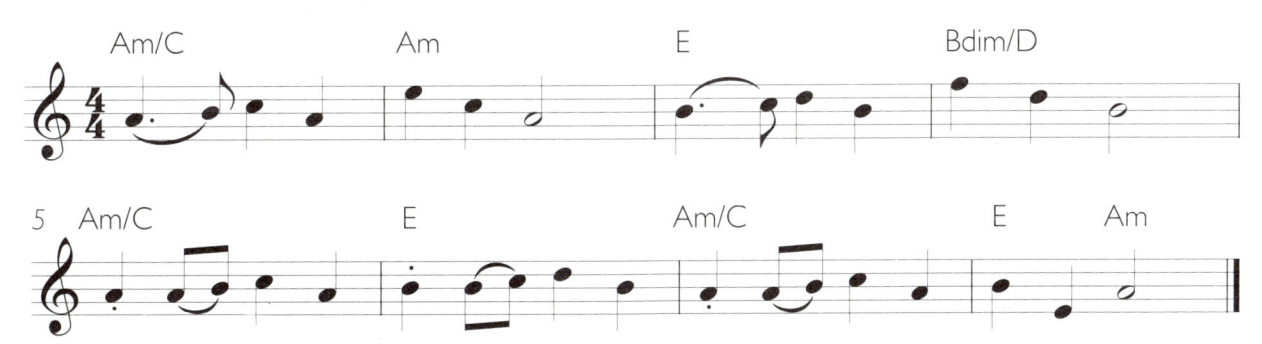

COMPOSING
27

We can then add a second part using devices such as imitation, sequence and inversion and performance detail (e.g. dynamics and tempo indications) to make it into a more interesting piece.

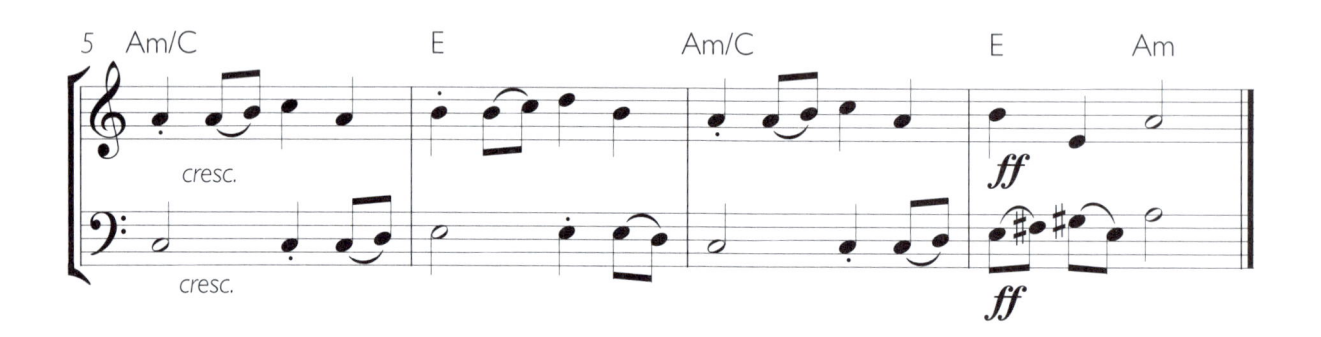

Here is a short example of what your piece might sound like:

CD3 Jeux d'Adresse

You have now looked at ways of developing and extending your compositions. These are just a few ways to do it – you need to experiment with your music to see what else you can do. You will earn credit in the final assessment for developing your ideas so you do need to work at it.

JEUX D'ADRESSE

Moderato   Peter Kay

Is the composition finished?

You have now developed an idea using various techniques and produced a fairly satisfying piece of music, but is it a finished composition? This is up to you! You could simply give the piece a title and leave it as it is. However, you could make it a part of a longer structured piece of music. It could be the first part of a ternary piece of music (ABA) - you could compose a 'B' section using similar compositional devices, then have the 'A' section repeated. You could use your music as a **rondo** theme (ABACADA etc.), with repeats of the theme separated by **episodes**, i.e. different themes of contrasting character. Once again, this is up to you - it is your composition (although you should ask your teacher for advice).

Review Details

- **Always experiment with your ideas**
- **Add second, third and even fourth parts to your melodies**
- **Arrange the parts so that the melody part isn't always played by the 'top' instrument**
- **Use rests**
- **Extend your composition using imitation, inversion, repetition and sequence**
- **Add performance detail – dynamics, tempo, instruments on which the music is to be played, etc.**
- **Always play your music and experiment with it – is there any more you can do?**

4. Ostinato

A lot of music is inspired by a story or a poem a composer has read or heard. A poster or painting, a film or newspaper article can spark off the imagination instantly.

In this section we are going to feature a poem and develop a new composition using a musical device called ostinato.

Ostinato is a constantly repeated short melodic phrase or rhythm. It literally means 'obstinate' or 'persistent'.

You can use an ostinato in several different ways. It often represents a repetition (e.g. a machine) or a continuous movement (e.g. the sea). It can be a very effective means of creating atmosphere and tension.

Try to create a simple melodic ostinato. Use only a few notes in your pattern and keep the notes close together. Build it up by recording your pattern several times and then introducing a new idea above it, with a second ostinato.

Try a rhythmic ostinato on untuned percussion instruments. You could start by creating a simple rhythmic pattern on side drum and introduce the tambourine, the cymbal with brushes, or guiro, using contrasting patterns. This could form the basis of your composition.

Here is a poem by Robert Louis Stevenson:

From A Railway Carriage

Faster than fairies, faster than witches,
Bridges and houses, hedges and ditches;
And charging along like troops in a battle,
All through the meadows the horses and cattle:
All of the sights of the hill and the plain
Fly as thick as driving rain;
And ever again, in the wink of an eye,
Painted stations whistle by.

Here is a child who clambers and scrambles,
All by himself and gathering brambles;
Here is a tramp who stands and gazes;
And there is the green for stringing the daisies!
Here is a cart run away in the road
Lumping along with man and load;
And here is a mill and there is a river:
Each a glimpse and gone for ever!

As you read this poem, you hopefully felt the rhythm of the train as it raced across the countryside. Today's trains still make a pleasing repetitive rhythm as they travel on the track. This is the sort of rhythm that could be referred to as an ostinato.

Read the poem again and see if you could think of a short phrase that could be repeated to represent the train on the tracks.

Try it on a drum. The rhythm of the train could be something like this:

Clap or play this rhythm as you count three in each bar.

Now you are going to add a simple repeating pattern of notes over your rhythm to represent the repetitive motion of the train:

The notes you have chosen suggest a minor key. Remember that the power of an ostinato is often what you add to it. This might be:

1. a further ostinato, gradually building up in layers to represent speed

2. adding a melody

3. changing the harmony while your ostinato continues.

Because the simple pattern of notes you have chosen is in the minor key, you have decided to use minor chords in your accompanying keyboard part. At certain intervals of time your chords will descend gradually and you can experiment with different chords against your ostinato.

Look again at the poem. What about the different scenes and objects that rush by? Would you want to represent them in your piece? You could try to introduce the occasional 'characters' as they appear in the poem.

How could the piece start? 'fairies' and 'witches'? A *flying* sound? Possibly glissando whistles, or trilling flutes diminuendo/crescendo?

'charging along like troops in a battle' Could a brass instrument, such as a cornet, represent the idea of soldiers?

'Painted stations whistle by' What happens to sound when an object 'whistles by'? The sound gets lower in pitch. What instrument could represent this? Possibly a glissando on the trombone?

'Here is a cart run away in the road' Perhaps a small percussion instrument representing a tin cup rattling against the cart as it bangs down the road?

'Each a glimpse and gone for ever' Does the ostinato of the train on the tracks start to disappear into the distance? (diminuendo)

You can see from these ideas how you can musically develop features from this poem.

Try creating your own piece using some of these ideas. You may find you see the poem quite differently and want to emphasise different lines. Decide on the form of the piece:

1. how it starts

2. what other features appear during the piece

3. how it ends.

It might be wise to have the ostinato playing throughout the piece with parts added or subtracted.

Your choice of instruments is important. Make sure you are using contrasting sounds so that individual parts can be heard.

When writing this piece out you may be able to employ simple signs and drawings for your players, rather than strict notation. You may also be able to direct or conduct the performance live. Here is an example of how your parts could be written:

side drum

keyboard

cornet

synth. effects

trombone

PIANO RANDOM ASC: NOTE CLUSTERS

COMPOSING

Here is an example on the CD of the sort of ideas we have suggested on the previous pages:

CD4 From a Railway Carriage

Review Details

- **Ostinato** – constantly repeated short melodic phrase
- **Rhythmic ostinato** – constantly repeated rhythmic pattern
- **Ground bass** – constantly repeated theme or passage in the bass part
- **Diminuendo** – the music gets gradually quieter
- **Establish** your ostinato, before adding other parts
- **Experiment** with different textures/sounds to achieve good balance
- **Look** carefully at the poem to see which lines are important
- **Write** your ideas down so that they are understood by other players

5. Improvise

Improvising means creating music 'on the spot'.

Improvising is just about as old as time itself. Long, long ago players would communicate across the land – 'talking' to each other in rhythmic phrases, altering and repeating the patterns and adding variations. This was one of the earliest forms of improvising.

Bach, Mozart and Beethoven were excellent improvisers and gave performances often improvising on their own compositions, by request from their enthralled audiences.

Sadly, improvising has all but died out in Western classical music. Fortunately this is not the case in other cultures such as in India and the Far East, where this form of music-making is very important. It is also not the case as far as jazz, rock and folk music are concerned, where improvising is alive and as popular as ever.

The most common method of improvising is creating a melody over given chords. Sometimes in rock and folk songs, you will hear an 'instrumental' improvised on the chords. This has the effect of creating variation to the song. It also gives a player in a group a chance to show off her/his individual skills and gives a singer an opportunity to improvise around the lyrics.

How to improvise

Individuals improvise in different ways because improvising depends on:

- **the instrument played**
- **the standard played to**
- **the individual's understanding of chords and harmony**

Here are three ways to develop your improvising skills:

1. **clapping rhythms**
2. **playing musical patterns**
3. **adding a melody to given chords**

1. Clapping rhythms

This is a good way to develop your improvising skills. You alter rhythms 'on the spot' to create balanced patterns within a four-beat framework. Try this with a friend. Here are four rhythms. Clap each one and ask your friend to repeat it after you.

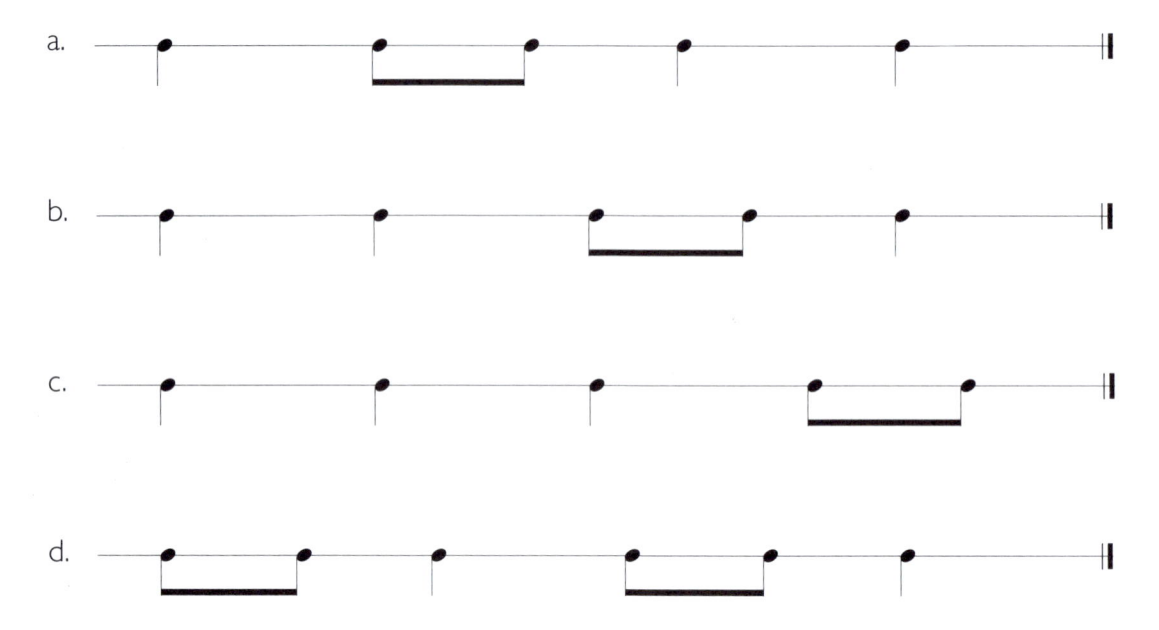

a.

b.

c.

d.

Now let's try to improvise. Ask your friend to clap each rhythm again. 'Answer' the rhythm you hear with a different four-beat rhythm. In your answer, try to use similar rhythms, for example:

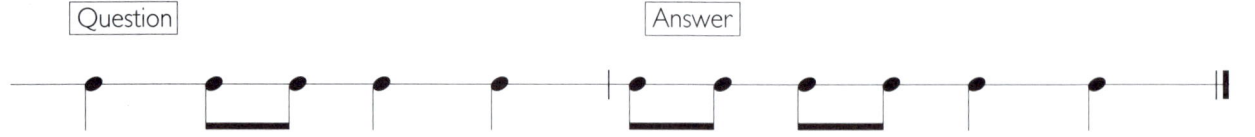

Question   Answer

These are called 'question and answer' phrases: you're talking to each other without saying a word!

Now try different question and answer rhythms, adding semiquavers (♬♬) and dotted crotchets with quavers (♩. ♪). Keep the beat slow enough so that you can cope with the different rhythms.

2. Playing patterns

This is very similar to clapping rhythms, except you use pitch as well as rhythm. You can do this exercise alone or with a friend. Here are melodies (or 'questions'). First play each melody. Now give an 'answer' to each 'question'. For example:

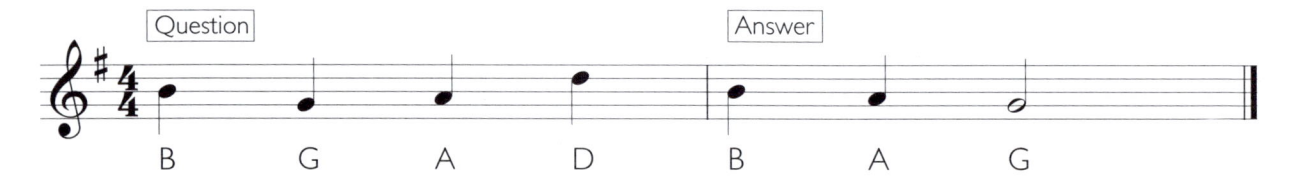

Question   Answer

B G A D   B A G

GCSE MUSIC

Make your answer simple and balanced, keeping the range of notes roughly within the
notes given in each question. Each example is in the key of G.

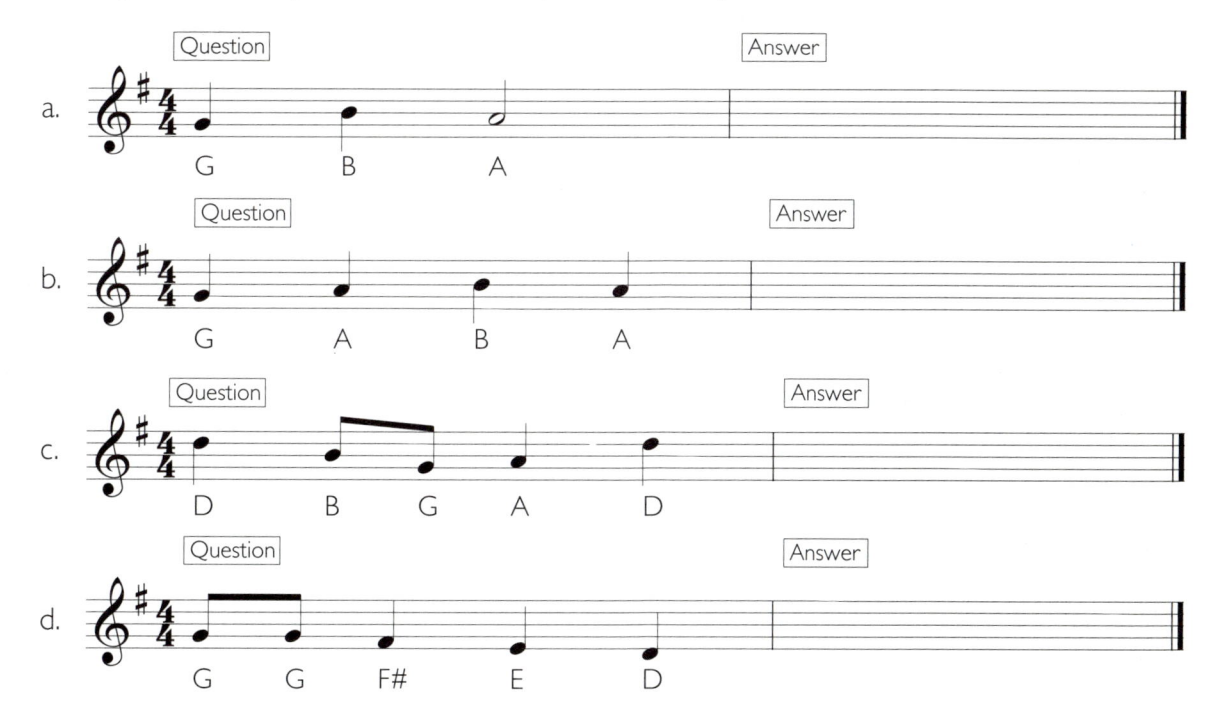

a.
Question: G B A | Answer

b.
Question: G A B A | Answer

c.
Question: D B G A D | Answer

d.
Question: G G F# E D | Answer

3. Adding a melody to given chords

You have successfully created rhythm and melody in a 'question and answer' form.
Now go one step further: take a melody and a set of simple chords and attempt to
improvise on them in the same 'question and answer' form. The piece *Conversations*
comprises a four-bar introduction, followed by patterns of two bars of melody with
chords and two bars of chords only.

In each of the two bars with chords only, you are going to improvise. Listen to the
piece on CD5, following the music on page 38.

CD5 Conversations

CONVERSATIONS

You can now:

a. **play the piece as a keyboard piece, attempting to add your own melody in the empty bars**

b. **record the chords into your keyboard, and then improvise on the melody**

c. **have a friend play the accompaniment on a 'chord' instrument, while you add the melody**

d. **play your instrument along with the band on the CD**

e. **best of all, try a selection of these, varying your improvisation each time!**

Just before we start, let's consider what is going to help you create a successful improvisation:

1. **learn carefully the given part by listening to the CD a few times**

2. **keep your improvised passage in a similar style**

3. **use similar rhythms and range of notes to those given, or it will sound disjointed**

4. **think about the shape – will you use longer notes at the end of phrases – how can you make it sound finished?**

5. **enjoy it!**

Extension work

You are now going to improvise on the following melody with given chords.

ODE TO JOY

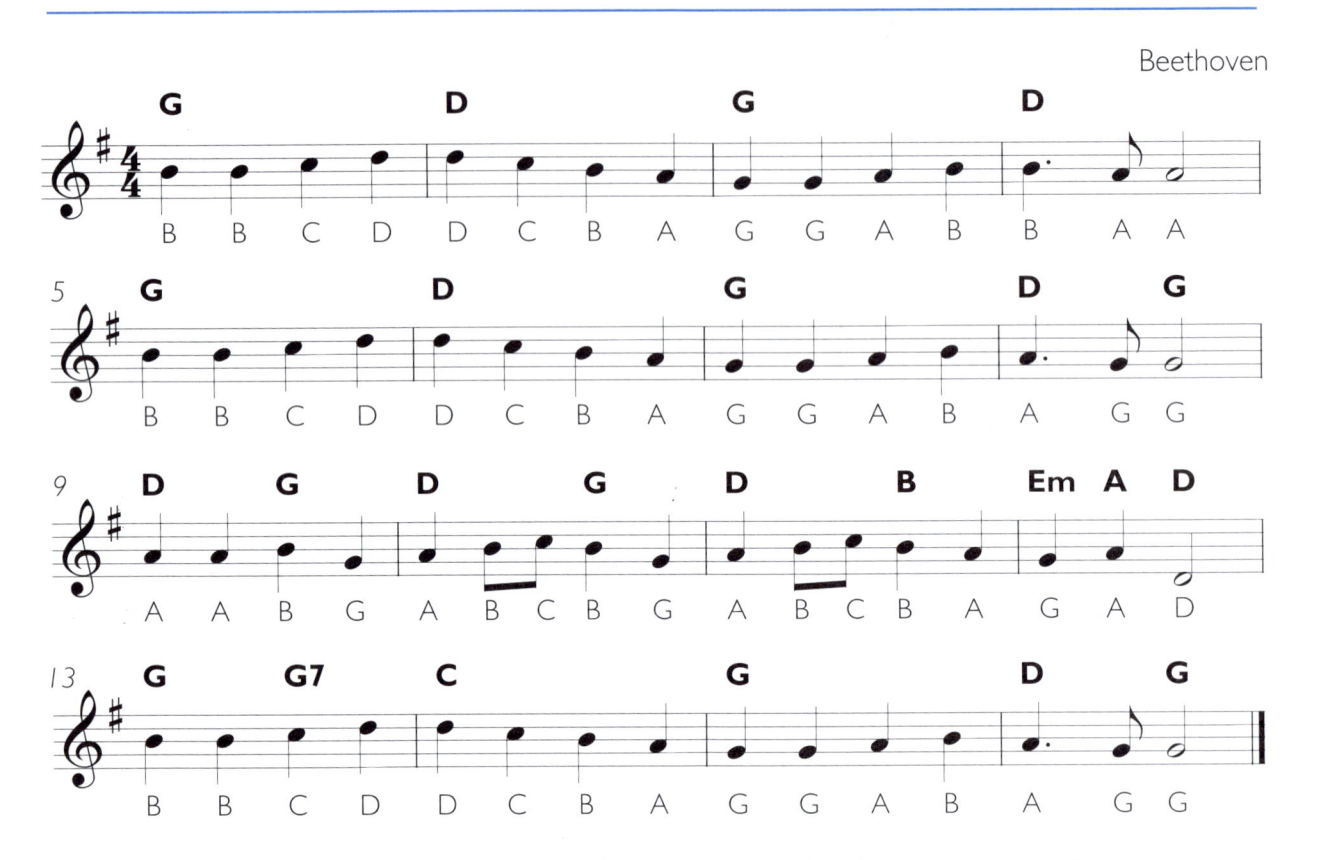

Beethoven

G	D	G	D
B B C D	D C B A	G G A B	B. A A

G	D	G	D G
B B C D	D C B A	G G A B	A. G G

D G	D G	D B	Em A D
A A B G	A B C B G	A B C B	A G A D

G G7	C	G	D G
B B C D	D C B A	G G A B	A. G G

The music is written out as a melody with single finger chord names printed above the music.

Now listen to the arrangement of Beethoven's *Ode To Joy* on the CD. A further three playings of the arrangement follow without the melody. There is one bar of four beats between each playing.

CD6 Ode to Joy

Use the CD as an accompaniment or use the written chord names if you wish to play the accompaniment.

Additional tips before you begin

1. **Think of your improvising as 'talking'. You talk using groups of words to form phrases.**

2. **Listen to the chord progression. It will suggest where longer notes will be required.**

3. **Listen to the melody a few times and think how you will alter it. Here are a few ideas:**

- **repeat given notes**
- **make first notes in the bar longer, missing out other melody notes**
- **miss out the first note of each bar**
- **add broken chords**
- **play the melody up or down a third at chosen places**
- **add in notes, e.g. the key note G**
- **introduce ornaments (quicker notes around the given melody)**

Use your imagination to think up your own ideas. Keep them simple and remember you're not trying to create a completely new tune. Your first attempts may be very similar to the given melody, but you will become more ambitious!

Review Details

- **Improvising** – creating music spontaneously (usually means creating a melody over given chords) – used extensively in jazz, and also in folk, rock, and world music
- Keep your improvisation within the genre (style) of the music
- Make sure your ideas are simple at first
- Record your work, or it may disappear for ever!
- Further help in *Writing it Down* section on pages 50 to 56

COMPOSING

6. Words

Songwriting is another way of composing music. As with any kind of composing, it takes practice to become good at songwriting. Many of the world's greatest songwriters are self-taught, and have their own very personal way of working. There is no set magic formula for writing songs.

However, it is helpful to break down a song to see how it is constructed. You can then use some of these construction techniques to create your own songs.

Some composers add words to a given melody, while some words and music are written at the same time (simultaneously). The most common way to write a song is to add music to words that have already been written.

Choosing the lyrics

The first thing to do when writing a song is to be very careful about the words you choose. Bear in mind the following points:

1. **Make sure you like and understand the words.**

2. **Avoid famous poems: adding music will probably not enhance them – they are famous and successful in their own right as poetry!**

3. **Read through the words carefully. Do they have a natural rhythm, a shape that is going to allow you to add a balanced melody line?**

4. **What kind of words appear in the lines? Are they going to be attractive or awkward words to sing? Do they flow with similar sounding words? For example, 'a quaint old cottage in the country' is far easier to write a melody for and sing than 'a scrap heap of rubbish propped up the derelict building'!**

5. **Read the words aloud. It's not how they look, but how they sound that matters. Look for the possibility of sequence (the same pattern of notes, repeated up or down a step), and repetition (repeating patterns of notes) where lines of words rhyme, or are similar. Sequence and repetition are good techniques to bind your melody together, making it strong and convincing.**

We have chosen these lyrics:

More Than Words Can Say

There is something in the way you say hello
Something in the way you smile
If there's one thing in this world that you should know
I couldn't leave you even for a while
In the rain and snow of winter
In my cold and darkest day
There is something in your eyes that always shines
It's more than words can ever say.

Getting an idea

Now that we have decided to use the verse from *More Than Words Can Say*, we have some very important decisions to make.

Forget about the choice of key, speed and instrumentation for the moment. It's time to experiment.

Idea >>>>>>>> Develop >>>>>>>> Complete

Look again at the lyrics. You may be able to sing the first line right away. This often happens: you see the rhythm of the line, and a simple melodic pattern comes to you.

If so, play or sing these notes until you are sure you have them. Scribble them down, or tape them, as you are certain to forget them. You have an idea!

If you haven't been so lucky, that's OK. You should continue to experiment using voice or instrument – the way you doodle with a pencil – trying things out, scoring them out, trying them again. Look at the rhythm of the first line. Say the words, clap the beat.

If nothing has come yet, go to the keyboard. Create a single finger chord rhythm, fairly slow. Put together a couple of bars of chords, say D and G, four beats each. Try a simple pattern of notes that will fit the first line, either by playing or singing. It doesn't have to be a classic melody!

You now have some sort of melody line. You could work on and see where it gets you, writing a little bit down at a time.

If these efforts have not worked, a more structured approach like the one on page 44 will be of benefit to you. The lyric content suggests a fairly happy, romantic, easy-going melody. A march or a jig would not be suitable!

Working out rhythm

Let's consider the rhythm. Read the verse aloud, placing a line between the words to represent bar lines like this:

```
    *        *         *    *       *     *    *    *       *
There is / something  in the  way   you   / say  he- llo

      *        *       *      *      *       *     *
   / Something  in the   way    you /  smile
```

As you say the lyrics, accent (make louder) the underlined words as you clap (*). Look at the words which occur before the first underlined word – 'There is'. We will add an **anacrusis** (a melody note played before the first full bar) to them.

There are four beats between these underlined lyrics, so we will have four beats to each bar. Using the above system, let's now add the rest of our 'beats', decide on our bar lines, and add rhythm to the lyrics.

Again, go back to saying the words aloud to decide on the particular rhythm. This should reflect the natural rhythm of the lyrics.

Take particular care to identify syllables – you will need a note for each of these. The rhythms used for syllables (and small words) are often quicker. At the end of line 4, and at the end of the verse we may wish to have longer pauses to reinforce the general shape of beginning, middle and end.

Here then, is the layout we have chosen for the basic rhythm of the verse, with bar lines added.

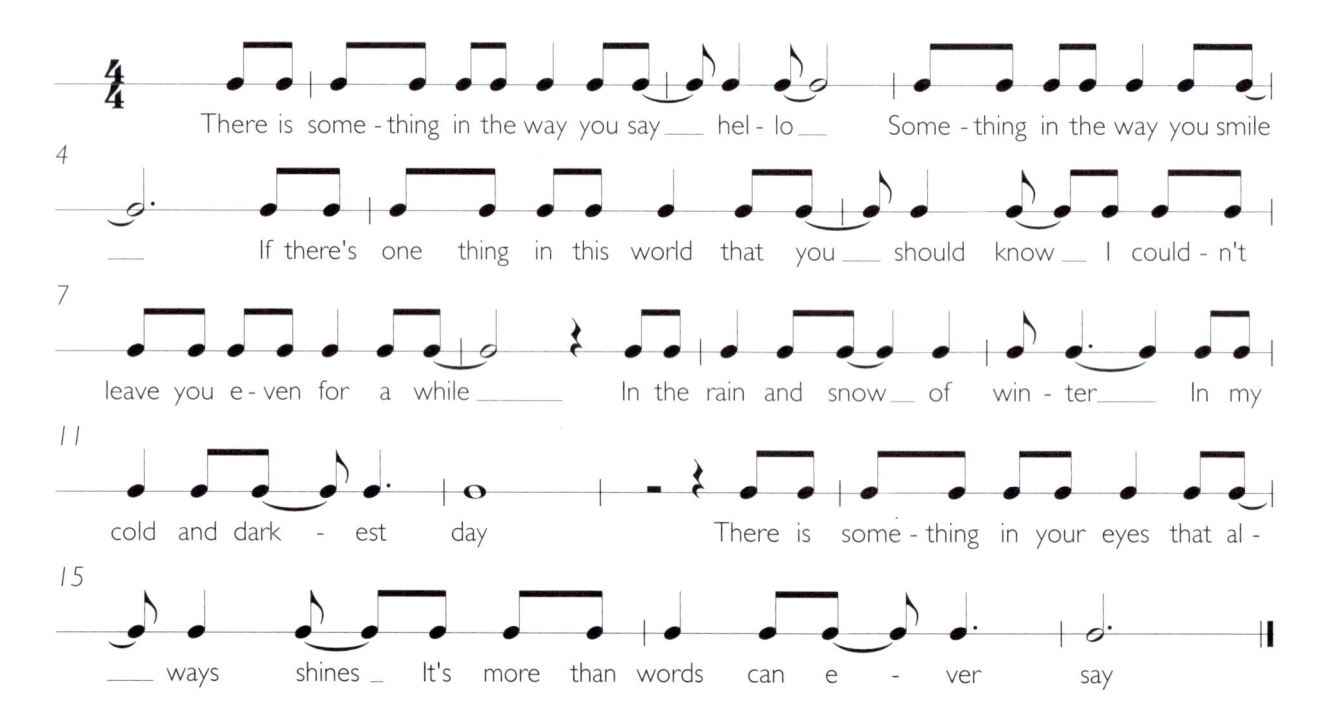

There is some - thing in the way you say ___ hel - lo ___ Some - thing in the way you smile

___ If there's one thing in this world that you ___ should know ___ I could - n't

leave you e - ven for a while _____ In the rain and snow ___ of win - ter ___ In my

cold and dark - est day There is some - thing in your eyes that al -

___ ways shines ___ It's more than words can e - ver say

Writing a melody

The lyrics dictate the way we construct the melody, so return to the verse to see how it has been put together.

Looking again we can see that lines 1 and 2, and lines 3 and 4 take on the simple structure of question and answer.

A statement is made (line 1), and the statement is answered (line 2) and so on. The shape of this pattern is reinforced with lines 1 and 3, and lines 2 and 4 rhyming. This is all good news for the composer!

Balanced rhyming lines create opportunities to use **sequences** and repetition.

Let's try and put some melody together, bearing these points in mind. We have experimented with a few notes beginning with D, E and F#. Let's look again at our chosen rhythm.

When we come to our first 'strong' word (in this case 'something'), we want the melody note to help to establish the key.

After experimenting with the first line lyric, we have come up with this melody phrase, suggesting the key of D major. The first 'strong' word will sound on an F#, part of the chord of D, our key chord. We will 'push' or **syncopate** some notes in the rhythm to give the song a 'natural' feel – look at the words 'say' and 'smile' – they enter *before* the start of the new bar.

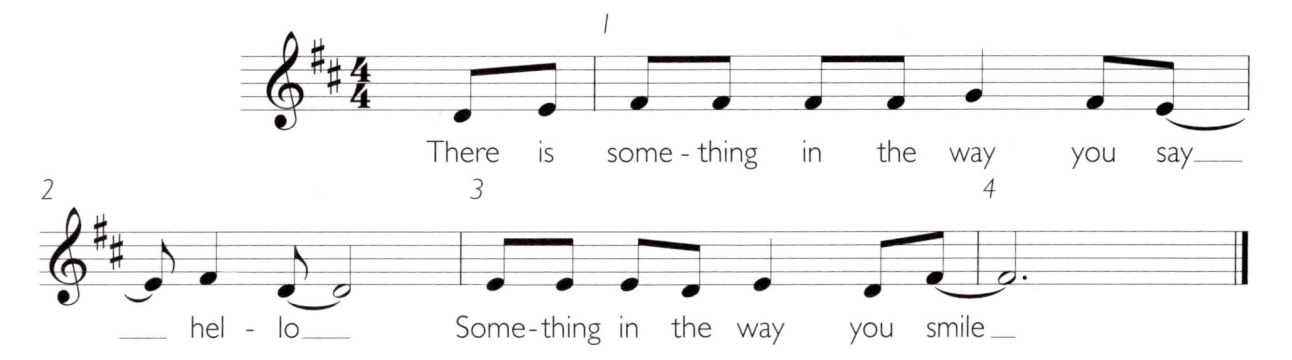

Bars 3 and 4 answer bars 1 and 2, so we suggest a sequence which fits the lyrics.

Having established this part, we are now well on our way with the melody. The hardest bit is over.

Now go on and look at bars 5 to 8. We can see that the rhythm of the words is very similar to bars 1 to 4. So we can virtually repeat the musical phrase, altering it at the end to suggest the use of chord V – or 'A'. Here we have an 'E' note in the melody which is part of the 'A' chord.

[Musical notation, bars 5–8: "If there's one thing in this world that you should know I couldn't leave you even for a while"]

Look now at bars 9 to 12. Something different is required here. We need to get away from the format of the first 4 lines, or the song could suddenly become a bore!

For these lines it would be wise to extend the range of the melody. After trying out several notes a little further up the scale, we have decided upon this phrase, making sure it is still in singing range:

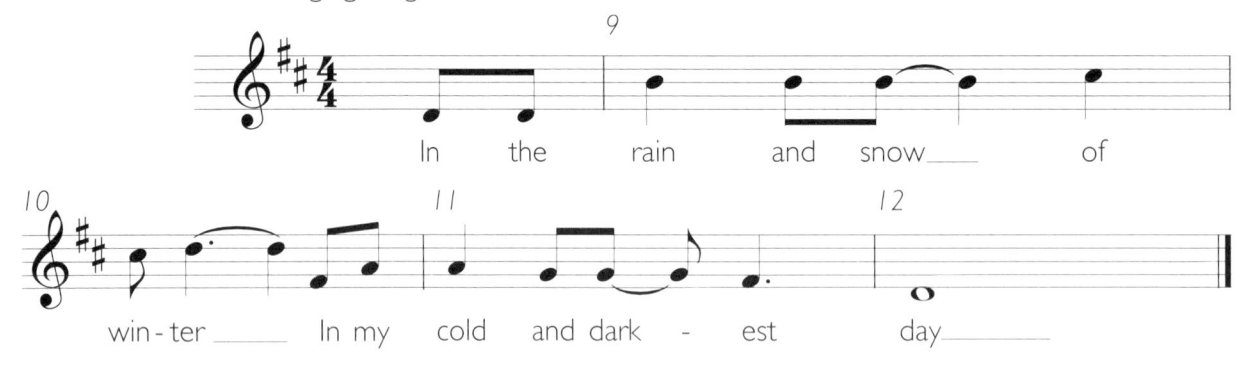

[Musical notation, bars 9–12: "In the rain and snow of winter In my cold and darkest day"]

At the end of these lines we also want to prepare the listener for a return to the melody introduced in line 1.

It would be good for lines 7 and 8 of the lyrics (on page 43) to be like lines 1 and 2. Why?
Because they are similar in word content (repetition) and we want to give the song *shape* by reintroducing the phrase we used at the beginning.

In this way we produce a balanced piece, using our chord progressions sensibly.

Adding chords

Having tried a few chords it is agreed we are in the key of D major. The range of notes we have been working around will suit the singer's voice. We are going to use the famous chord progression I, IV, and V (in the key of D major, the chords of D, G and A).

When we come to the 'halfway point' (bar 9) of our verse we do not want our piece to sound finished, so a good tip is to go to the chord of V (A in this case). The ear now expects to hear more.

We are also going to add three more chords: E minor as a substitute for G, to add interest, and B minor to give us a contrasting chord; we will also include the chord of G minor, as an interesting substitute for G before we restate the opening phrase to bring the verse to a close in the home key.

Use the expertise of your teacher to help you understand the many areas covered here. Remember that this is only one way of songwriting – you may have a completely different method that works for you.

As in other kinds of composing, listen to plenty of songs, to their chords, and to their shape. You'll learn a lot by listening.

You can hear this song on CD7 (the music is on page 49). Try to play it or sing it with a friend.

CD7 More Than Words Can Say

Extension ideas

On CD7 you heard a recording of *More Than Words Can Say* for voice and keyboard.

On CD8 we have extended the composition by:

1. **Adding an introduction. Look for a simple motif or riff (short pattern of notes which appear in the piece at various points) which you could use as an introduction. This could be a few notes which already occur in your song.**

2. **Adding an instrumental. Adding a verse of 'solo' or lead instrument and improvising over the verse chords.**

3. **Arranging. Based on your original accompaniment, create parts for guitar, bass and drums, possibly with a 'solo' instrument. Which players are available in class? This could make an interesting group performance!**

4. **Improvising. By altering the melody line rhythmically, by adding syncopation and by experimenting with chords.**

5. Adding a harmony. Experiment with different vocal harmonies. Singing notes a third apart from the melody will often sound good.

6. Adding a coda (an additional passage at the end to 'round off' your song).

CD8 More Than Words Can Say (extended)

Review Details
- Take care in choosing your lyrics
- Take care with range of notes used
- Use your teacher's expertise – there's a lot to learn
- Listen to other composers' work
- Sequence – a pattern of notes repeated usually up (or down) a step
- Anacrusis – a note (or notes) at the beginning of a piece before the first full bar
- Chord Progression – the particular order of chords

MORE THAN WORDS CAN SAY

John Montgomery

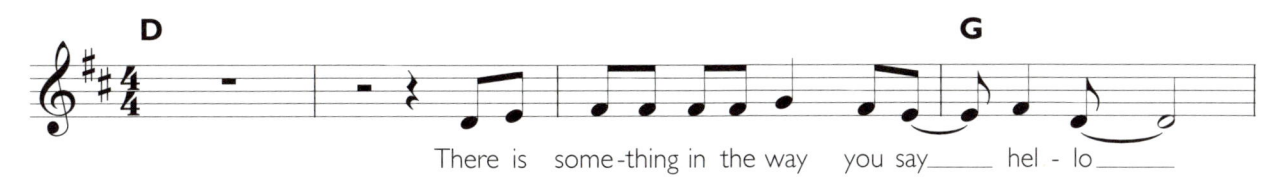

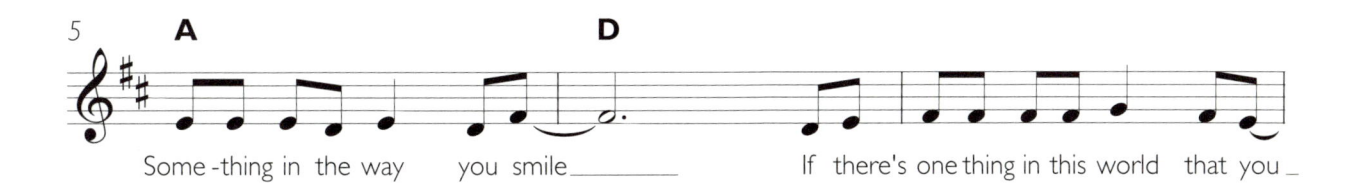

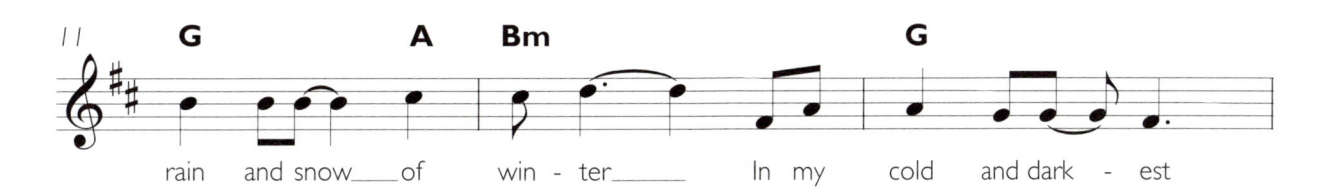

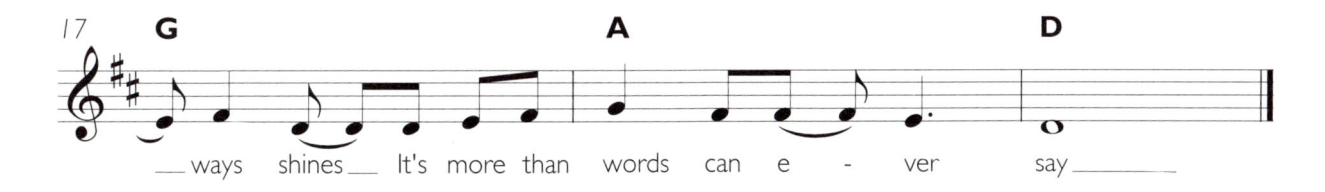

There is some-thing in the way you say___ hel - lo___
Some-thing in the way you smile___ If there's one thing in this world that you___
___ should know I could-n't leave you e - ven for a while___ In the
rain and snow___ of win - ter___ In my cold and dark - est
day___ There is some - thing in your eyes that al -
___ ways shines___ It's more than words can e - ver say___

COMPOSING
49

Writing it Down

This section offers you some help in writing your compositions down. It will help you understand the words and signs commonly used in written music.

Recordings of your composing work on tape should match your written performance plan. If your piece is going to be recreated or performed at a later date using other players, then you have to write your instructions down in a way that they will understand.

You may write your music in picture form like this:

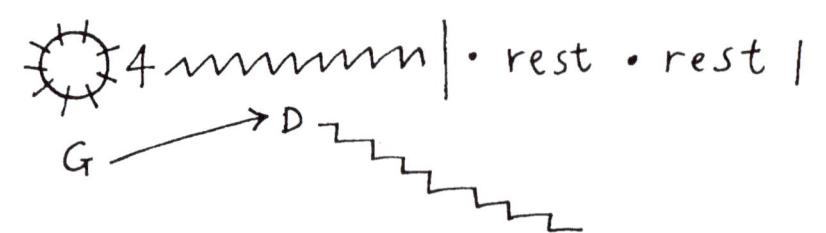

Or you may use note names with bar lines and note lengths like this:

You may have your own very personal way of recording your instructions on paper – this is fine, as long as it can be understood by others.

Conventional notation

This is the system of writing down music that has been in use for hundreds of years. If you use this system, your work can be recreated and understood immediately by other players who can read music.

Here is the information you need to know to write down your music. You can refer to this when you want to write down a composition, and you can use it for instrumental parts when preparing your Composing tape.

Treble Clef (most 'smaller' instruments use this clef)   Ledger Lines

One Octave

C D E F G A B C D E F G A B C
(middle)

Note that semitones occur (marked as ⌒) between B and C, and between E and F.

Bass Clef

A B C D E F G A B C
(middle)

Here is one way to help you remember the notes:

Lines (Treble Clef):

E G B D F

Every   Good   Boy   Deserves   Fun

Spaces (Treble Clef):

F A C E

Lines (Bass Clef):

G B D F A

Good   Boys   Deserve   Fun   Always

Spaces (Bass Clef):

A C E G

All   Cows   Eat   Grass

COMPOSING
51

Rhythm and rests

Simple time:

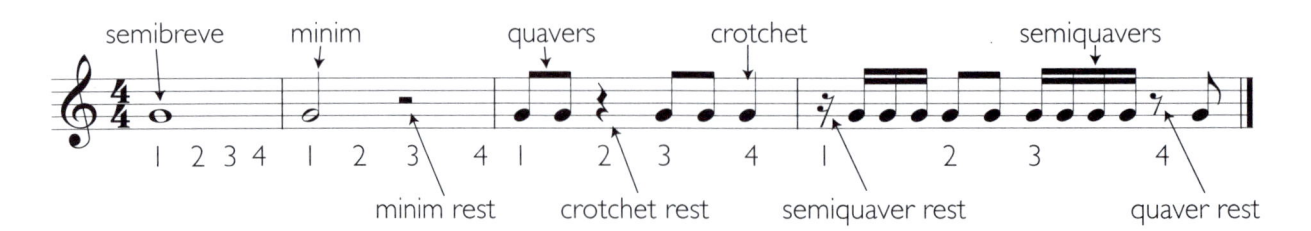

[Musical notation showing: semibreve, minim, minim rest, quavers, crotchet rest, crotchet, semiquaver rest, semiquavers, quaver rest — in 4/4 time]

Compound time:

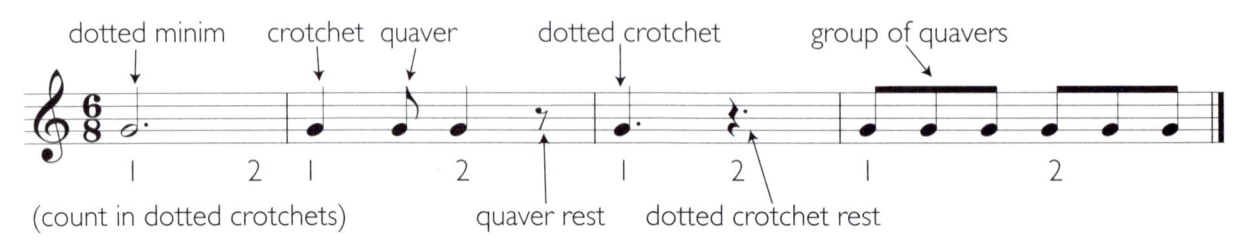

[Musical notation showing: dotted minim, crotchet, quaver, quaver rest, dotted crotchet, dotted crotchet rest, group of quavers — in 6/8 time]

(count in dotted crotchets)

Keys

Music is written in different keys in order to obtain a particular sound, or to suit a particular instrumental range (e.g. the clarinet's). The key signature (sharps or flats at the beginning of each line of music) tells you which key the music is in. This ensures that every key uses the same system of tones and semitones.

Here are the most common keys used to write compositions in. Every major key has a relative minor key (the major key and its relative minor use the same key signature) as below:

C Major/A Minor   G Major/E Minor   D Major/B Minor   A Major/F# Minor   E Major/C# Minor

F Major/D Minor   Bb Major/G Minor   Eb Major/C Minor   Ab Major/F Minor   Db Major/Bb Minor

Chords

You can use chords to harmonise your melodies. You can play chords in different positions and you should experiment with them. Playing a chord using the same notes in a different position (or order) is called an inverted chord.

Here are the most common chords:

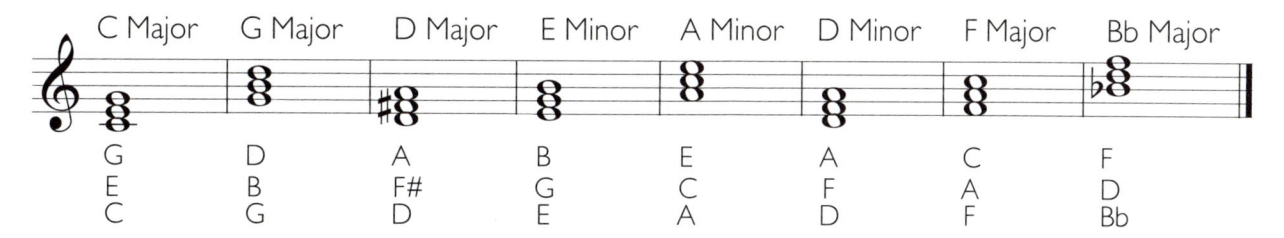

C Major	G Major	D Major	E Minor	A Minor	D Minor	F Major	Bb Major
G	D	A	B	E	A	C	F
E	B	F#	G	C	F	A	D
C	G	D	E	A	D	F	Bb

Here are the common chords you would use in the following keys:

Chords commonly used to accompany a melody in C major:

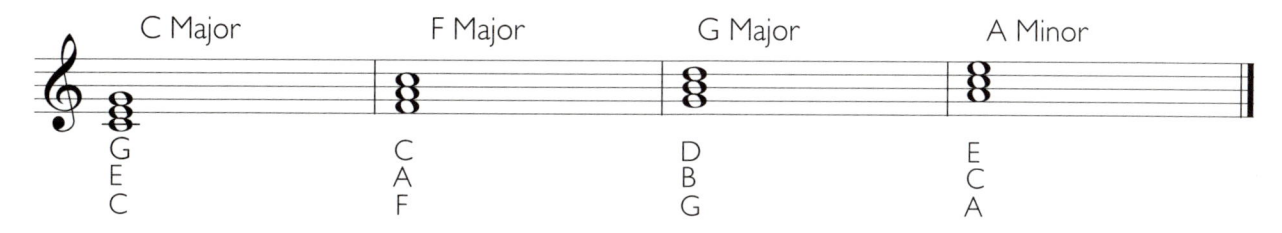

C Major	F Major	G Major	A Minor
G	C	D	E
E	A	B	C
C	F	G	A

Common chords in F major:

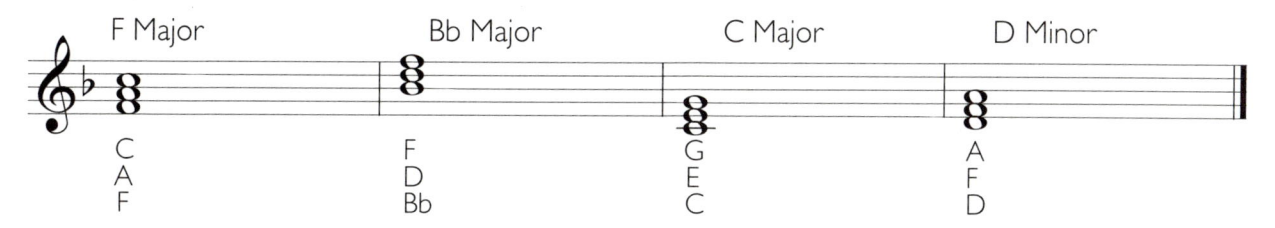

F Major	Bb Major	C Major	D Minor
C	F	G	A
A	D	E	F
F	Bb	C	D

Common chords in G major:

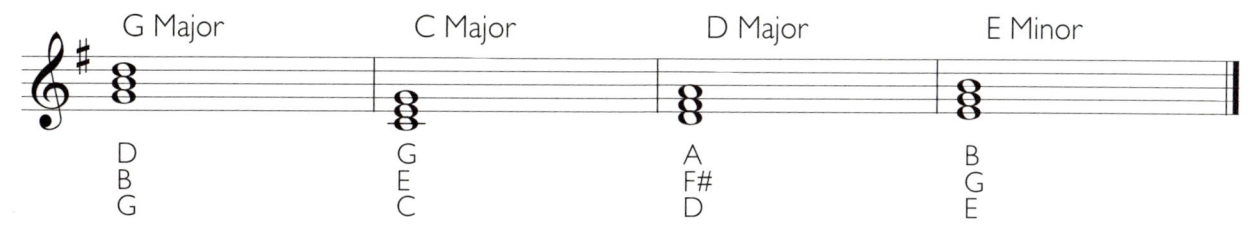

G Major	C Major	D Major	E Minor
D	G	A	B
B	E	F#	G
G	C	D	E

COMPOSING

Common chords in A minor:

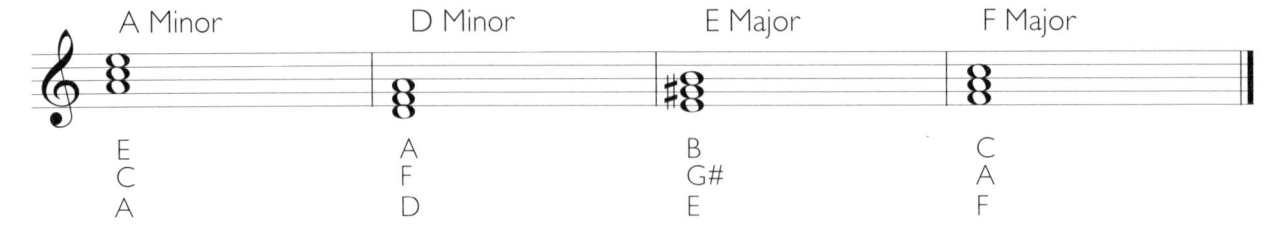

A Minor	D Minor	E Major	F Major
E C A	A F D	B G# E	C A F

If you are playing a keyboard instrument, you could add the note name of the chord with your left hand and play the note lower down the keyboard (e.g. add the note G in the left hand with the chord of G in the right hand).

Guitar and bass guitar players sometimes use a system called Tab (short for tablature). Tab is a picture of the guitar strings with the numbers written on a particular string to match the fret on the guitar. If you need an open string played, you would use the letter O, writing it on that 'string'. Here are a few notes written in notation and altered into Tab:

Melody A:

Converting notation to guitar tablature:

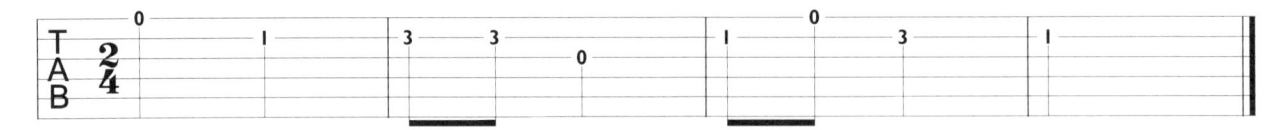

Melody B:

The bass guitar has only four strings and would look like this in Tab:

Guitarists also use guitar 'windows' to read chords. This time a picture of the neck of the guitar shows the strings in an upright position, with the first few frets added. Here are 8 popular guitar chords:

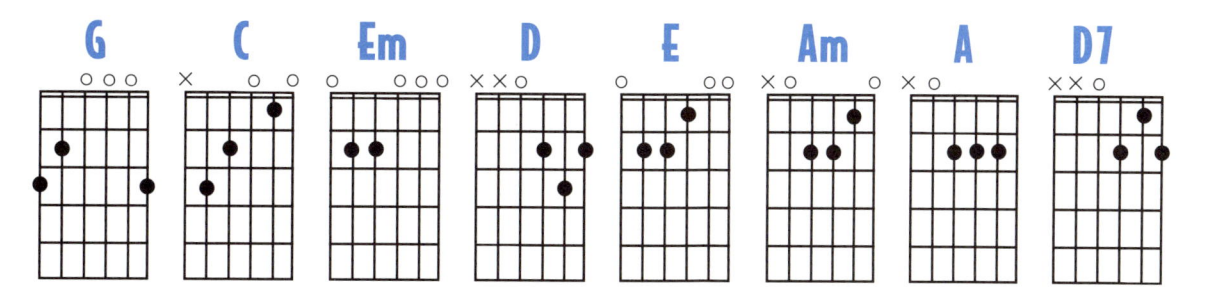

G   C   Em   D   E   Am   A   D7

x = don't play these strings
o = play as open strings

Transposing instruments

If you create a piece for a clarinet, a trumpet, a french horn or an alto saxophone, for example, then you will have to **transpose** the music. This means that you will have to write it in a different key if any of these **transposing instruments** are to play in the same key with other instruments. The most common transposing instruments are 'Bb instruments':

Trumpet	Baritone	Cornet	Euphonium
Clarinet	Trombone (treble clef)	Tenor Saxophone	

For these instruments you have to write the melody up one tone for it to sound correct.

Here is an example.
Melody in the key of F major:

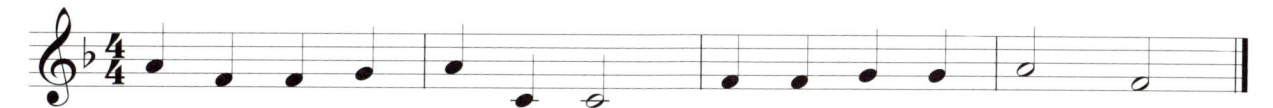

Transposed for Bb instrument (to *sound* the same as above):

COMPOSING

The french horn (and cor anglais) are 'F instruments'. Music for these instruments has to be written up a perfect fifth or down a perfect fourth (you have to decide which of these will make the melody fit the instrument better). The melody on page 55 would look like this when written for an 'F instrument':

Alto saxophones and tenor horns are 'Eb instruments'. Music for these instruments has to be written a minor third down (or a major sixth up) like this:

Your teacher will help you with written parts which need to be transposed.

Tempo

To state the tempo (speed) you want a piece played, you could write one of the following Italian words at the beginning of your music:

lento (very slowly)

adagio (slowly)

andante (at a walking pace)

moderato (moderately)

allegro (quickly)

presto (very quickly)

vivace (fast and lively)

LISTENING AND APPRAISING

LISTENING AND APPRAISING

Introduction

The listening and appraising element of GCSE Music gives you a great opportunity to experience a wide range of musical styles. During your course, you listen carefully to music, discuss and then answer questions on what you hear. Listening and appraising also helps you with your composing and performing.

At the end of the course you take an examination in which you listen to several extracts from different styles of music and then answer questions about them. These may be related to specific areas of study. Some of these questions will be multiple choice; for others you will need to give short written answers.

This section includes details of the different styles of music you need to be able to recognise.

In the exam, you will be asked to listen to a piece of music and identify:
- a) the type of ensemble playing (e.g. choir, orchestra, string quartet, rock group)
- b) the type of piece (e.g. opera, concerto, pop song)
- c) the historical period (e.g. Baroque, Classical, 20th Century)

You may also be asked to suggest a possible composer and to give reasons for your suggestions. Study the table of composers on page 59. It will help you answer this kind of question.

Table of Composers

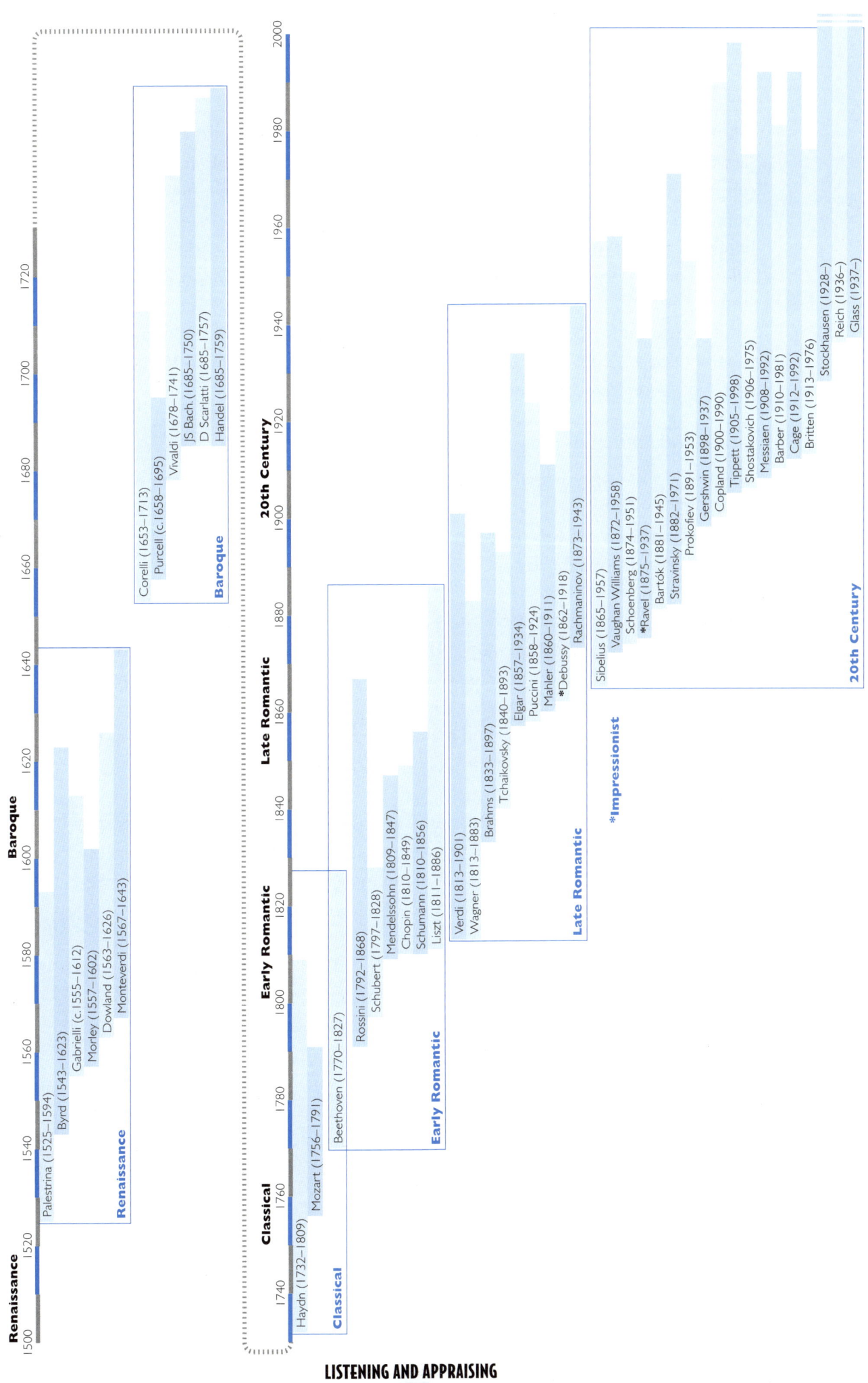

Renaissance
1500 — 1520 — 1540 — 1560 — 1580 — 1600 — 1620 — 1640

- Palestrina (1525–1594)
- Byrd (1543–1623)
- Gabrielli (c.1555–1612)
- Morley (1557–1602)
- Dowland (1563–1626)
- Monteverdi (1567–1643)

Renaissance

Baroque
1640 — 1660 — 1680 — 1700 — 1720

- Corelli (1653–1713)
- Purcell (c.1658–1695)
- Vivaldi (1678–1741)
- JS Bach (1685–1750)
- D Scarlatti (1685–1757)
- Handel (1685–1759)

Baroque

Classical
1720 — 1740 — 1760 — 1780 — 1800

- Haydn (1732–1809)
- Mozart (1756–1791)
- Beethoven (1770–1827)

Classical

Early Romantic
1800 — 1820 — 1840

- Rossini (1792–1868)
- Schubert (1797–1828)
- Mendelssohn (1809–1847)
- Chopin (1810–1849)
- Schumann (1810–1856)
- Liszt (1811–1886)

Early Romantic

Late Romantic
1840 — 1860 — 1880 — 1900 — 1920

- Verdi (1813–1901)
- Wagner (1813–1883)
- Brahms (1833–1897)
- Tchaikovsky (1840–1893)
- Elgar (1857–1934)
- Puccini (1858–1924)
- Mahler (1860–1911)
- *Debussy (1862–1918)
- Rachmaninov (1873–1943)

Late Romantic

20th Century
1900 — 1920 — 1940 — 1960 — 1980 — 2000

- Sibelius (1865–1957)
- Vaughan Williams (1872–1958)
- Schoenberg (1874–1951)
- *Ravel (1875–1937)
- Bartók (1881–1945)
- Stravinsky (1882–1971)
- Prokofiev (1891–1953)
- Gershwin (1898–1937)
- Copland (1900–1990)
- Tippett (1905–1998)
- Shostakovich (1906–1975)
- Messiaen (1908–1992)
- Barber (1910–1981)
- Cage (1912–1992)
- Britten (1913–1976)
- Stockhausen (1928–)
- Reich (1936–)
- Glass (1937–)

20th Century

*Impressionist

LISTENING AND APPRAISING

World Music

The term 'World Music' loosely covers music from around the world which is not the classical or popular music of the Western world. World Music is often very different from the music we are used to hearing. It isn't possible for you to listen to and study every type of music from around the world during your course. However, remember that every type of music is made up of patterns created through sound and silence. Different people organise the sounds in different ways and use different 'sound sources'.

In the Listening and Appraising examination you may be asked to listen to a piece of music and say where it might come from, describe the sound of the instruments or say what the 'World Music' influences are on a piece of popular music.

Indian and Pakistani music

Indian and **Pakistani music** includes most types of music on the Indian sub-continent. There are variations in music throughout this large area, just the same as there are variations between music in different parts of Europe. However, there are some things which we can say about Indian and Pakistani music in general.

Melody is very important in these types of music. The music is not based on chord progressions as it is in Western music. The melodies are constantly changed through improvisation – often using intervals smaller than the semitones we are used to hearing in the West. The basic melodies are built up using **ragas** – these are ways of organising notes similar to major and minor scales. There are a great number of ragas, all designed to convey a mood or emotion (e.g. love, anger or devotion).

The rhythm added to Indian and Pakistani music is based on a pattern which is known as the **tala**. There are a great number of these also, each having a fixed pattern on which the performers improvise. Some of the most popular talas have 6, 10 or 12 beats in their cycle but many have more, and these are often subdivided.

The beautiful sound of the **sitar** is commonly heard. This is a complex instrument to master; it has a small body, a large neck with moveable frets and usually seven strings – with two of them acting as a **drone**. The sitar is often accompanied by the **tabla** – a pair of single-headed drums of different sizes.

Improvisation is a key part of Indian and Pakistani music. Added to the fact that there are so many ragas and talas, and that no type of music stops evolving or changing (especially with the influences of Western music), you will find that there is much variety and interest in Indian music.

Listen to these examples. CD track 9 is from India and CD track 10 is from Pakistan.

> **CD9 Bangla Dhun (Shankar)**

> **CD10 Sab Vird Karo Allah Allah (Ali Khan)**

Indonesian Gamelan

Further east to islands such as Bali and Java, we find another fascinating sound, that of **Indonesian Gamelan**. Gamelan is the name given to the Indonesian ensemble (group) made up of percussion instruments – different-sized metallic instruments similar to glockenspiels and metallophones. These are sometimes accompanied by untuned drums and occasionally a **suling** (a flute-like instrument).

The music is based around a single melody which is developed and improvised upon at different tempos by the members of the group (or orchestra). The music is arranged in pitch layers. The result is a mesmerising and delightful experience where all the parts come together as one.

Listen to this example:

> **CD11 Gending Langiang (Sekehe Gender Bharata Muni)**

Some very famous Western composers such as Debussy, Glass and Reich have been influenced by Gamelan.

Latin American music

For rhythmical excitement and the joy of dance it is hard to equal the tantalising sounds of **Latin American music**. This is the term used for music from South America. Here we find percussion of all shapes and forms whose roots we can trace to African drumming. The influences of music from South America can be seen in the salsa-based popular Western music today.

South America is a large continent and, as we would expect, there are many different types of music heard there. The syncopated **samba** from Brazil with its easy $\frac{2}{4}$ timing and the rhythmical songs and dances of the **salsa** (originally from Cuba – an island which is heavily influenced by South America) are very infectious and are an important part of everyday South American culture.

Pan pipes also form a distinctive part of the South American sound in countries that border the Andes such as Chile and Peru. Music heard in these countries is largely based on the traditional music of the Aztecs and Incas. However, the Latin influence can also be heard in a lot of music played in the region. This is particularly evident when the evocative sound of the pan pipes is combined with the small guitars which have been developed from instruments brought to the area by the Europeans in the 16th century.

Listen to this example, where influences can be heard from South America and Europe:

CD12 Un Aeroplano A Vela (Testa/Ponzo)

The Latin music which we immediately associate with Brazil and the surrounding countries has influences from the South American Indians and the European colonisers, as well as from the African slaves brought to the area. The result is a rich and lively musical heritage which has affected (and has been affected by) much of today's music.

Listen to these tracks:

CD13 Fato Consumado (Djavan)

CD14 La Bamba (Gomez-Orozco)

Caribbean music

In the past, the **Caribbean** was colonised by many different European countries including Spain, Portugal, England, Holland and France. These countries' cultures have all influenced Caribbean music. Perhaps more important, however, are the influences from Africa, again as a result of the huge number of African slaves brought to the islands.

Music from this area tends to be based on quite simple chord patterns and repeated syncopated rhythms such as:

These rhythms are used a lot in **calypsos** and **mentos**, many of which you may have sung. Here are some examples of songs to which you can add the above rhythm:

- **Linstead Market**
- **Hill an' Gully**
- **Jamaica Farewell**
- **Humming Bird**
- **Banyan Tree**

The steel pans have become associated with the region since the end of the Second World War. They were originally constructed from abandoned oil drums and have now become a part of the musical culture of the region, being used to play all kinds of music.

Music does not stop evolving. Many musical cultures can be combined to produce some very interesting results. For example, we have already seen that salsa has affected popular Western music.

Listen to these tracks, and notice the varied influences that you can hear:

> **CD15 Jump for Joy (Lyons/Lewis)**

> **CD16 Trinidad Farewell (Arconte)**

African music

Africa is a vast continent and there are many different styles of music reflecting its many different cultures.

Although there are a great number of instruments used in Africa, two of the main sound sources are the drums and the voice. The rhythms used often seem complex to those unused to hearing them. Sometimes, the main beat of the music is in the body movements which accompany and are part of the music. Against the beat, several layers of sound are built up, often creating a three-against-two rhythm. Often, the different rhythmic lines seem to be at different speeds making the music sound even more complex.

There are many different types of drum used in Africa including **tama**, **dundun**, **kalengu** (hourglass-shaped drums) and **djembe** (goblet-shaped drums). They may be played with sticks, hands or a combination of both. Many of the drums are tuned to various pitches and may be accompanied by a **balafon** (a xylophone-type instrument). All of these instruments are constructed from natural materials.

As well as singing songs, performers often imitate the sound of instruments and amplify their voices using animal horns or shells. Sometimes, the voice is used to add to the rhythms created by the drums.

Listen to this example:

> **CD17 Dance of the Woman**

West Africa is reputed to be the home of many of our popular styles of rock, reggae and blues. Look again at the section on Blues on pages 20 to 24 and we can see the connection – millions of West Africans were shipped to the Americas as part of the slave trade, bringing with them their ancient musical traditions.

Just as with all music, African music continues to evolve and both affects and is affected by Western popular culture.

You can hear African influences in this track produced in Britain:

> **CD18 Serengetti (Quin)**

Far Eastern music

Japan, **China**, **Vietnam** and **Korea** are geographically very close to each other. Because of this, the music from each of these countries has been influenced and continues to be influenced by all the others. All the music in this region is basically pentatonic, but intervals of less than a semitone are often used to decorate the music (as in the music of India). Much of the music is **heterophonic** which means that there may be several different instrumental lines to the music but each instrumentalist plays the same basic melody. Each performer develops and decorates the melody in her/his own way. There is a method of writing down this type of music. However, as most melodies are learned and developed by each performer, the written music is only used as a guide.

The instruments used in the various countries are also similar, although they are given different names. The instruments are designed to imitate the sounds of nature. The Chinese **ch'in** consists of strings (usually made of silk) stretched over a wooden soundboard. The strings are plucked. The soundboard is marked to allow the performer to stop the strings to alter the pitch. The similar Japanese instrument is the **koto**, the Korean instrument the **kum** and the Vietnamese instrument the **dan tranh**. There are also flutes and drums which are similar throughout the region.

However there are differences in the music of each of these countries. For example, in China, vocal music has a particular place. Buddhist chants accompanied by bells, gongs and cymbals are still heard in the temples. Stories are still told to the accompaniment of music. The Chinese Opera has become a highly stylised form where folk legends and stories of wars are related using music, dance, drama, acrobatics and elaborate costume and make-up. In Japan, the Shinto (Japanese religion) chants date back to the 1st century. Chinese Buddhists introduced their chants to Japan in the 4th century and the two types of chant co-existed from then on. **Gagaku** is a type of Japanese music which was performed especially for the nobility and has remained virtually unchanged for hundreds of years. Here is an example of Gagaku:

> **CD19 Rokudan**

What You Should Know

- **Balafon** – an African xylophone-type instrument
- **Calypso** – Trinidadian folk music often with words related to topical, even political issues
- **Ch'in** – a Chinese plucked string instrument usually with silk strings
- **Dan tranh** – a Vietnamese plucked string instrument
- **Djembe** – an African goblet-shaped drum
- **Dundun** – an African hourglass-shaped drum
- **Heterophony** – type of music where there are several instrumental lines playing the same basic melody but each one decorates or develops the melody in their own way
- **Kalengu** – an African hourglass-shaped drum
- **Koto** – a Japanese plucked string instrument
- **Kum** – a Korean plucked string instrument
- **Mento** – Jamaican folk music including different types of song and dance
- **Raga** – scale or mode on which Indian melodies are based
- **Suling** – an Indonesian flute-like instrument
- **Tala** – Indian rhythmic pattern
- Other highlighted words in this section (check glossary)

Ragtime – Concepts at Work

Ragtime is a particular style of composition. It was very popular first in America and then in Europe in the early 1900s. This was mostly due to the young American composer Scott Joplin who wrote many Piano Rags, and made the style his own. His most famous is *The Entertainer*. Ragtime died out in the early 1920s, giving way to popular jazz.

Many people think that ragtime was an early style of jazz but as you listen to and study this piece called *Sweet Talkin' Rag*, you will realise that the two styles have little in common. Jazz is the art of improvising while ragtime is rhythmically very strict, almost march time with regular melodic lines, and occasional syncopation. The majority of ragtime compositions were written for the piano.

Listening for compositional features and devices

In the examination you may be asked to identify 'compositional features' or 'compositional devices' when you hear a piece of music. Many of these 'devices' are used in all types of music. Study the *Developing Ideas* section on pages 25 to 30.

Follow the music of *Sweet Talkin' Rag* on pages 67 and 68 while listening to it on CD track 20. Several words and phrases have been added in boxes to help you understand the meaning of the music. You may have to listen to this track a number of times to be able to understand all of the features and devices included, but don't worry about this – in the examination you will hear each extract for this type of question at least three times.

CD20 Sweet Talkin' Rag

SWEET TALKIN' RAG

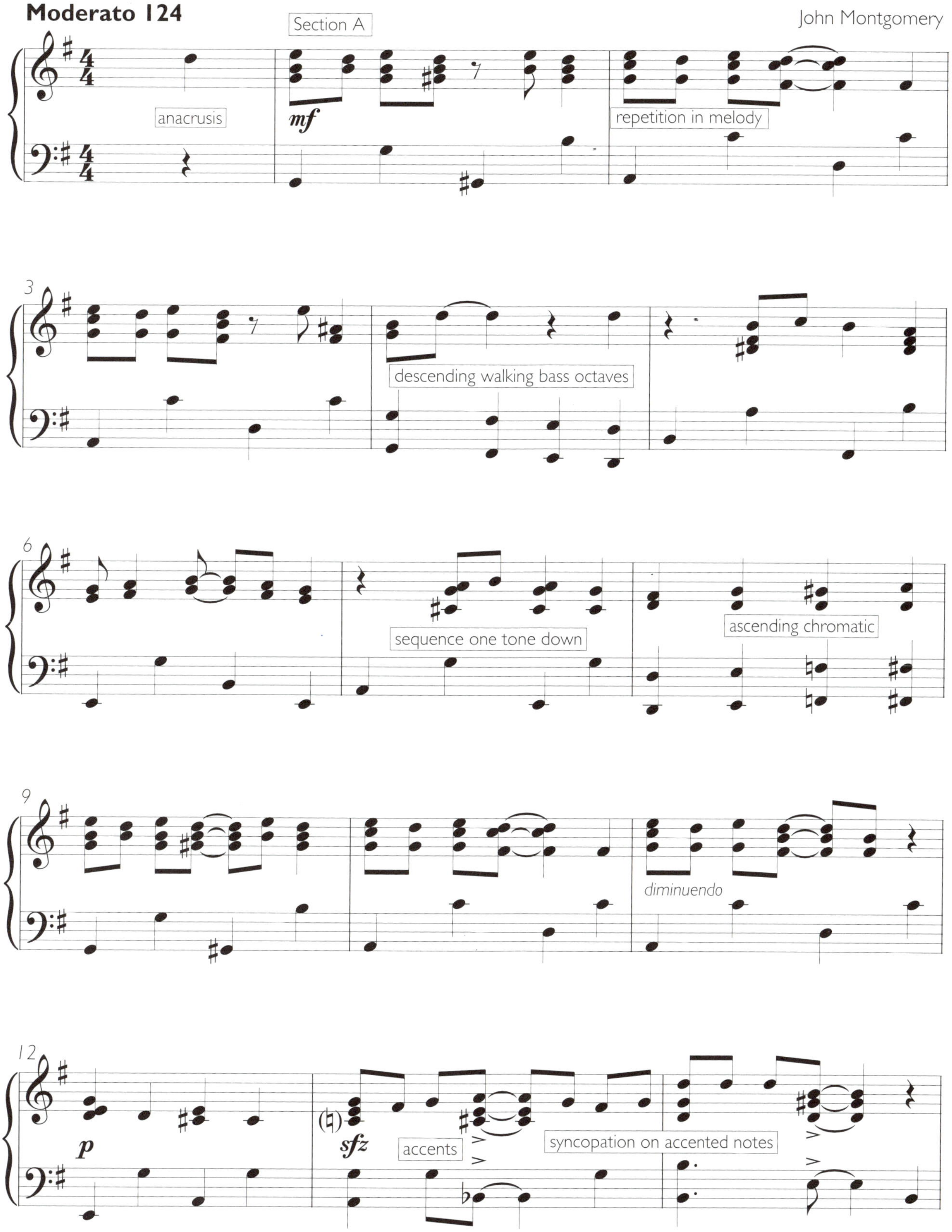

15
Section B
mf
melody in bass in steps
19
accompaniment in upper parts
p
mf cresc.
sequence down one step in bass melody
23
Return of Section A
modulation to dominant
f
mp
27
interrupted cadence
cresc.
f
31
Coda
mp
ff
diminished broken chord
34
diminuendo
mp
perfect cadence
pp

Here are some features and devices which are used in *Sweet Talkin' Rag*:

- **Key G major**
- **Speed – moderato (at a moderate pace)**
- **Time signature – strictly four beats to the bar**
- **Special features – syncopation, chromatic notes, modulates briefly**
- **Form – Ternary (ABA) with a Coda**

Bar 4

Descending walking bass (A bass part which moves down in steps.) This one is also in octaves (notes with same name eight notes apart).

Bars 5–7

Sequence (A group or phrase of notes repeated usually up or down one step.) A good device to strengthen your compositions! Sometimes the pattern, as in this case, is not exactly the same.

Bars 13–14

Accent (Where notes are accented or played louder than others – marked > above or below the accented note.)

Bars 13–15

Syncopation (Where the natural stress or pulse has been moved.)

Bars 21–24

Modulation (To suggest a new key by introducing a note or chord, not part of the key you are in – in this case note C#.) This C# is, however, in the key you are suggesting (in this case D major).

Bar 33

Coda (A passage added to the end of a piece of music to give it a strong sense of ending.)

Bars 35–36

Cadence (A harmonic figure, usually the combination of two chords at the end of a section or phrase.) This one is a **perfect cadence** and gives a 'final' sound, using the chords V to I.

See if you can find other bars where any of the above occur.
Check in the glossary for words mentioned in the music, but not explained above.

LISTENING AND APPRAISING

> **What You Should Know**
> - Ragtime – dance music popular in the 1900s – mainly piano music with syncopated melody and steady march-like accompaniment
> - All concepts featured in music including expression marks
> - For explanation of words not explained look up the glossary

The Voice

The human voice is a musical instrument, with the added advantage of sounding words at the same time as producing notes.

A massive amount of music has been written for voice through the ages, and today the song remains the most powerful musical form. For hundreds of years the church was the central source for musical composition and performance.

By listening to music from different centuries you can identify musical progression and development. A thousand years ago a single line of music would be harmonised in parts which usually moved in parallel motion and at the octave. This was called organum. The music would be unaccompanied and in 'free rhythm', without bar lines. Often the use of melisma, or a **melismatic** effect (singing more than one, or indeed several notes on the same syllable) would be employed, for example, in ancient music of Christian worship. The opposite effect (that is, of always singing one note for one syllable) is called **syllabic**.

From these early forms, part-writing and **polyphonic** ('many-sound'/'many-voice') choral writing developed. Byrd and Palestrina, and later Bach, used polyphonic techniques to great effect in their music. **Homophonic** (parts moving together 'hymn-like', with little or no individual rhythmic interest) is the opposite of polyphonic.

Vocal compositions are often **unaccompanied**. The term used to describe unaccompanied singing in the church is '**a cappella**' ('in the chapel style').

Voice ranges and word setting

Four distinct voice ranges make up a typical mixed choir:

- **Soprano (upper female voice)**
- **Alto (lower female voice)**
- **Tenor (upper male voice)**
- **Bass (lower male voice)**

Additional voice ranges (e.g. mezzo-soprano) can also be used. 'Mezzo' means 'halfway between'. So a mezzo-soprano voice is halfway between the soprano and alto range. A countertenor voice has a range higher than a tenor, while a baritone has a range sitting between the tenor and bass.

The way that vocal compositions are constructed is very important. **Word setting** (the way in which the words are placed into the music, and the effect created) has a huge influence on the interpretation of both the words and the music in a particular piece. Certain other effects can be achieved, for example by using **word painting**. This is an effect which composers use to describe a passage of words in musical terms, e.g. a story about a train journey could be described by the snare drum beating out the rhythm of the train as it crosses the sleepers. More instruments are added to represent the gathering speed of the train. See the section on Ostinato on pages 31 to 34.

Oratorio

In the 1600s, a musical composition called the **oratorio** was developed. An oratorio is a religious work for soloists, choir and orchestra, structured in many separate musical items, like an opera but without scenery or costumes. Oratorios would be performed in church and in concert halls. A **passion** is similar to an oratorio except it features the crucifixion of Christ as its central theme. The **cantata** is a similar composition but can also be of a secular (non-religious) nature. Here is an example from a very famous oratorio, *The Messiah* by Handel. One of the features of this music is the excellent use of **imitation** amongst the choral parts:

> **CD21 The Hallelujah Chorus – from The Messiah (Handel)**

LISTENING AND APPRAISING

Opera

This is a very important part of the vocal repertoire. There are several different types of opera, but most are large compositions performed on stage using costumes and scenery. There is usually an overture (a piece of music played at the beginning by an orchestra, introducing many of the themes you hear later as songs in the opera).

There are three main types of vocal composition the composer uses to tell the story: **arias** (complete songs for soloists); **recitative** ('sung speech' used to move the story on); **chorus** (where the main body of singers perform, 'commenting on' or reinforcing the story line).

Many famous operas have been written in Italian, by composers including Rossini, Puccini, Verdi and Mozart.

In the following aria (CD22) from a very popular Puccini opera, listen to the typically simple accompaniment where the strings share the soprano's melody line and the harp gently plays **arpeggios**. Listen to the changes in speed: this is called **rubato** ('robbed time') and is used by the composer in this typically **Romantic** work to add expression.

> **CD22 O Mio Babbino Caro – from Gianni Schicchi (Puccini)**

Musicals

These have many similarities to opera. The story, however, is often told using the spoken word (instead of sung 'recitative') and they are generally more light-hearted than opera. Musicals were first produced in 20th-century America.

In the past twenty years the British composer Andrew Lloyd-Webber has written several worldwide smash-hit musicals including *Cats*, *Phantom of the Opera* and *Evita*. Some of the more recent musicals have abandoned the spoken word and returned to the operatic notion of recitative, e.g. *Les Misérables*.

The 20th century has seen an explosion in popular music and song that can be traced back to African music. Different pathways have emerged. Pages 73 and 74 comment briefly on the different styles of vocal music you need to be able to recognise:

Jazz

Blues songs are slow, sad Afro-American compositions usually based upon the 'twelve-bar blues' chords, often in $\frac{4}{4}$ time.

Dixieland is a traditional style of early jazz from New Orleans around 1920, with lively, syncopated rhythms. Instruments featured are clarinets, trumpets and banjo.

Boogie-woogie is a very special kind of piano jazz. The left hand plays a repetitive and constant bass line while the right-hand melody is improvised upon. Like the blues, it is often in a twelve-bar format, but is usually played at a much faster tempo.

Swing became popular in the 1930s. Swing Bands were large and usually included saxophones. Many of the compositions have a lazy rhythmic swing to them. The singing too has a smooth laid-back sound to it, often with a gentle **syncopation** (shifting the natural accent of the music), and the use of **chromatic** notes (notes introduced in the melody/harmony which do not normally appear in the key of the piece).

Latin American has many of the features of jazz rhythm and harmony, often with a quick tempo and an emphasis on **percussion** (with plenty of bongos and drum patterns). Latin American songs and dances include rumbas and sambas.

Jazz (contemporary) has become more complicated. It often shares similarities with some of today's classical music, as well as having elements of jazz's own past. Complex harmony and **cross-rhythms** (e.g. 4 beats against 5) are often present.

Rock & Pop

In the 1950s, teenagers found themselves with money to spend on records after the harsh years of the Second World War. Rock music developed from Rock 'n' Roll (lively three-chord song/dance music). The terms 'rock' and 'pop' cover a range of different styles now, and ever since the dance hit *Rock Around The Clock* in the late 1950s, rock and pop music have flourished.

The natural progression from Elvis Presley to The Beatles, to punk, heavy metal, reggae, house and dance means that the rock business is a massive and ever-changing industry. Here is a typical example of pop music with a little reggae flavour. Listen out for the **electronic drums** (rhythm machine) with plenty of **reverb** on the **lead vocals** and **backing vocals**:

CD23 Beautiful As You (A Montgomery)

Most rock compositions are songs. They follow a similar pattern consisting of melody with mainly 3 or 4 chords. They are usually **strophic** (the words of each verse change but the music remains the same), not **through-composed** (where the melody changes for each new verse or stanza). To add interest they may also **modulate** (change key), creating a climax towards the end of the song.

What You Should Know

- **Polyphonic** – two or more melody lines of equal importance weaving together
- **Homophonic** – 'hymn-like' – all parts move rhythmically in step
- **Imitation** – a musical idea in one part is immediately repeated in another
- **Arpeggio** – a broken chord
- **Reverb** – an electronic effect used on microphones/electronic instruments
- **Electronic drums** – a computer-generated drum part, in which speed and drum fills can be programmed in
- **Lead vocals** – singer singing the main/melody line in a band
- **Backing vocals** – the voices that support/accompany the lead vocal line
- The different voice ranges
- The different vocal compositions – oratorio, opera, cantata, musical
- The different vocal compositions within the opera, e.g. aria
- Recognising the various song compositions/techniques
- Check highlighted words in the glossary at the back of the book

Music of the 20th Century

'Music of the 20th Century' refers to the classical music of the century, and not other styles (such as jazz or rock). Hundreds of magnificent classical works have been written in the 20th century. You'll be listening to a few of them on the CD.

Many 20th-century composers, including Stravinsky, Bartók, Britten and Prokofiev, have not yet fully enjoyed the recognition their music deserves. Such is the way with composers – they are often far ahead of their time, and it takes the rest of us many more years to understand just what they are getting at!

Several concepts in your course refer to 20th-century music and so this is a very important part of the Listening element.

In the late 1800s, great change and experimentation was taking place in composing. The **Romantic** Period was drawing to a close.

Impressionism is the name that was given to a style of painting popular in France in the second half of the 19th century. Monet, Degas and other Impressionists used the textures of light and tone hinting at, rather than stating in detail, the scenes and subjects they painted.

In the same way, some composers including Debussy and Ravel tried to write music to describe a given moment suggesting, rather than constructing, large-scale thematic frameworks (like many of the earlier Romantic composers).

Whole-tone scales, **glissandi** and **chromaticism** are musical devices commonly used in the works of Debussy, as you can hear from this extract from *Prélude à l'après-midi d'un faune*. This particular piece is considered to be the 'gateway' composition to the new music of the 20th century. Listen carefully to the way in which Debussy 'tone-paints' with the 'solo' woodwind instruments, including flute, clarinet and oboe:

> **CD24 Prélude à l'après-midi d'un faune (Debussy)**

An important and powerful work of the 20th century is Stravinsky's ballet *The Rite of Spring*. When it was first performed (in 1913) there was a public outcry – such were the shouts of disapproval from many members of the audience that the ballet dancers were hardly able to count to the music. This work uses many of the musical techniques which characterise the 20th-century music that followed. In this extract listen for **discords** in the harmony, **ostinati** and **atonality**. The changing bar lengths and powerful **syncopated** rhythms and **cross-rhythms** from the orchestra give the work great originality and 'savage primitivism'. Listen also to the way in which Stravinsky uses the instruments in a **percussive** way, e.g. **col legno** (with the wood of the bow) in the string parts:

> **CD25 The Rite of Spring – Dance of the Young Girls (Stravinsky)**

In the early 1920s, the composer Schoenberg structured his system of **atonal** music (music not in any key) which he had developed several years before. This system was based around the twelve notes of the scale being laid out in a particular order or 'row'. The order of notes could then be played in different ways, e.g. backwards, inverted (turned upside-down), and so on. This 'twelve-note system' became known as serialism.

Others looked to the past when composing new works. Prokofiev and Stravinsky were sometimes labelled neoclassicist because they based some of their compositions on the harmony and forms employed by earlier classical composers such as Mozart. You can hear the close reference to the classical period in this example by Prokofiev (CD 26). The orchestra scoring (similar to that used in Mozart's time) and the importance of the string section is clear. The structure of the music is heavily dependant on arpeggio and scale passages in the **minor** key, as well as on repetition and sequences. The piece still creates a great sense of freedom and originality, which is one of the reasons for its popularity.

> **CD26 Classical Symphony No. 1 (Prokofiev)**

Some composers, including Sibelius and Bartók, show a strong sense of nationalism in their music: they display a love for their countries and people through their compositions. In this extract from Bartók's *Music for Strings, Percussion and Celeste*, you can clearly hear a strong reference to Hungarian/Bulgarian folk music in the exciting rhythms and **syncopated** passages. This music is often atonal, and you can hear the use of **whole-tone** scales. Listen to the timpani and the way in which the piano is used as part of the percussion section.

> **CD27 Music for Strings, Percussion and Celeste (Bartók)**

What You Should Know

- **Impressionism** – style of music from late 19th-century France in which mood is hinted at rather than stated
- **Chromatic** – scale in semitones or notes added to melody; not part of the key
- **Whole-tone** – as in scale passage; there are no semitones, suggesting no key
- **Glissando** – to 'slide' ascending or descending across the notes
- **Percussion** – instruments which are struck (e.g. gong, timpani and xylophone)
- **Atonal music** – music not in any key, with no 'home' key
- **Tonality** – opposite of atonality; notes used in a particular established key
- **Ostinato** – a constantly repeated pattern of notes
- **Pedal** – usually bass note sustained or repeated while harmonies change above
- **Discord** – notes included in chords which do not normally belong
- **Romantic** – a 19th-century style of music after Classical

Shape and Form

Like poems and paintings and books and buildings, music needs shape and form. Shape and form give compositions purpose and direction.

When you read a novel you expect it to be complete and whole. Imagine your disappointment if the story line introduced early in the book disappeared in the middle, never to be heard of again. In music, composers use different forms and shapes to hold the listener's attention and to make the music complete and whole.

You may be asked to recognise elements of shape and form in your Listening exam. You will certainly come across different forms in all the pieces you play, and you may be able to learn one or two tricks for use in your compositions.

Binary form

This is a simple form which falls into two sections (A and B). The first section often **modulates** (changes key); the second section then winds its way back to finish in the original key. A popular example of binary form is *Good King Wenceslas*.

Ternary form

This is in three distinct sections (A, B, A). The first section is repeated for the third section, with a different section (B) in the middle. A good example of this is The Beatles' song 'A Day In The Life' (on the *Sgt. Pepper's Lonely Hearts Club Band* album). Look too at *Sweet Talkin' Rag* on pages 67 and 68 – another example of ternary form.

Canon

In a **canon**, one instrument or voice sings a part and is closely imitated, note for note, by another, starting later and overlapping the first voice. You can see that, if other voices are added in this way, a very complicated composition unfolds. Canon was used to great effect by Bach in his fugues (the strictest form of **contrapuntal** writing). A simpler form of canon is called a round or a catch. Try singing or playing *Three Blind Mice* in parts with a few friends to get the effect.

Listen to this fugue by Bach. In this composition from the **Baroque** period, you can clearly hear the 'voices' enter in imitation:

CD28 Fugue No. 16 in G Minor (Bach)

Minuet and Trio

This form was popular in the **Classical** period and is similar to ternary form. The minuet was originally a French dance with three beats to the bar. The trio was so-called because some early composers had only three instruments playing in this section rather than the orchestra. The trio eventually became known as Minuet 2, making the structure Minuet 1, Minuet 2, and Minuet 1. A good example of a Minuet and Trio is the third movement from Mozart's *Symphony No. 39 (K543)*.

Rondo

This was frequently used in the final movements of sonatas, symphonies and concertos in the **Classical** period. It is an extension of ternary form.

The rondo form is ABACAD and so on. A is the theme. Any sections which are not A are called **episodes** (contrasting sections in different keys). You can see that the theme (A) keeps recurring throughout the work. Mozart's *Horn Concerto No. 4* is a good example of a rondo.

> **CD29 Horn Concerto No. 4 – 3rd Movement (Mozart)**

Symphony

This is a large-scale work for orchestra, usually four movements in length. Composers of symphonies include Mozart, Beethoven, Tchaikovsky, Sibelius and Mahler. A symphony is normally described by number (in the order they were written), but occasionally also by name, e.g. Tchaikovsky's *Symphony No. 6 'The Pathétique'*.

Some music written in the 19th and 20th centuries is called **programme music**. This is music in which the composer wishes to convey a particular mood or emotion or suggest a particular landscape, event or story, e.g. Mendelssohn's *The Hebrides Overture*.

Concerto

This word has slightly different meanings, depending on what period of music is being referred to. For the last 250 years a concerto has meant a large piece of music for soloist and orchestra. A concerto usually has three movements, the second of which is slow.

Towards the end of the first (or last) movement it is common to have a **cadenza**. This is where the solo performer improvises in the style of the work, showing off her/his skills in a great flourish of notes. Most cadenzas are now written in by the composer. Again there is a huge choice of examples spanning hundreds of years. Here are a few world-famous concertos:

Mozart's Piano Concerto No. 21 ('Elvira Madigan')

Brahms' Violin Concerto

Elgar's Cello Concerto

Listen to the different ways the string instruments are played in Brahms' *Violin Concerto* on the CD. You can hear the **legato** (smoothly played) melody line against the **pizzicato** string accompaniment. This music was written in the 19th-century Romantic period.

> **CD30 Violin Concerto in D Major – 1st Movement (Brahms)**

...and finally

Listen to this music from 'Mars' (from *The Planets Suite*) by Holst written in the early 20th century. This is a good example of programme music. You can hear the rhythmic **ostinato** as the heavy accompaniment to the theme, representing the huge and ugly machinery of the war which was about to ignite across Europe in 1914.

> **CD31 Mars – from The Planets Suite (Holst)**

What You Should Know
- Modulates – where there is a change of key from that stated at the start of piece
- Programme music – describes a story, poem, place, etc.

Instrument File

Orchestral instruments

An orchestra is made up of four sections or families of instruments. (Instruments in brackets are not always used.)

SECTIONS	INSTRUMENTS	HOW THE SOUND IS PRODUCED
Strings 	violin, viola, cello, double bass, (harp)	**Bowing and Plucking** — with a bow sliding across the strings (**arco**), or plucked (**pizzicato**). They can also be played with the wood of the bow (**col legno**). Producing more than one note at a time (chords) with the bow is called **double-stopping**. Producing notes by a rapid back and forth movement of the bow (sounds continuous) is called **tremolando**, creating a trembling, atmospheric effect. **Vibrato** (fast and slight fluctuation between notes) is commonly used to add expression and create a 'singing' tone.
Woodwind 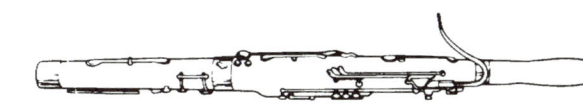	flute, clarinet, oboe, bassoon, (saxophone), (piccolo)	**Blowing** — using a single or double reed, except the flute and piccolo. A particular technique that wind players learn is **flutter-tonguing**, interrupting the stream of air to articulate notes (quickly repeating 'r' sounds creates the effect).
Brass 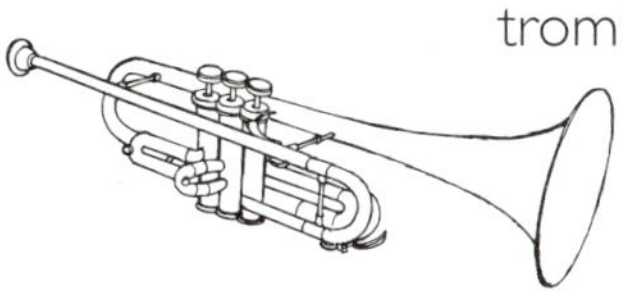	trumpet, french horn, trombone, tuba	**Blowing** — using valves, except the trombone which has a slide
Percussion: Untuned  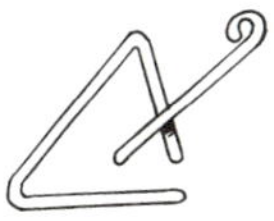	side drum, bass drum, cymbals, etc. 	**Striking** — using different kinds of beaters or sticks, or struck together, or hit by hand  
Tuned	xylophone, timpani, glockenspiel, etc. (instruments will vary depending on music)	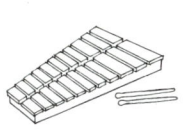 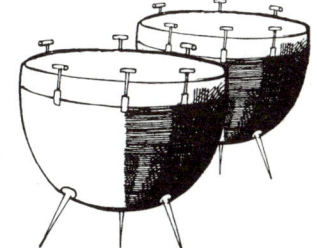

LISTENING AND APPRAISING

You can hear a selection of instruments featured on the following CD tracks:

CD22	harp	**CD28**	piano
CD24	clarinet, flute, oboe	**CD29**	french horn
CD25	bassoon	**CD30**	violin
CD27	timpani	**CD34**	saxophone

Apart from the orchestra, there are several other instrumental groups. Here are the main ones:

Military band

Made up of a selection of woodwind instruments, brass, and percussion. CD32 is an example of a military band. (They are now often described as concert bands.)

> **CD32 A Life on the Ocean Wave (Russell)**

Brass band

Unlike military bands, brass bands are made up solely of a large selection of brass instruments, often accompanied by percussion, but with no woodwind. Cornet (similar to trumpet), flugel horn, tenor horn and baritone are commonly used. CD33 is an example of a brass band.

> **CD33 Tritsch-Tratsch Polka (Strauss)**

Pipe band

Made up of bagpipes and drums (e.g. snare drums, bass drum).

Folk group

A selection of instruments (some traditional), depending on type of folk music played, including voice, fiddle (violin), clarsach (Scottish harp), acoustic guitar, whistle and accordion. Different cultures feature different instruments in their folk music, e.g. the sitar in India and the balalaika in Russia.

Jazz group

Usually features basic rhythm section of bass and drums, with either piano or guitar providing chords, vocals, 'lead' instruments such as saxophone, trumpet and clarinet. The selection of instruments in the group depends on the particular style of jazz being performed. CD34 is performed by a modern quartet consisting of saxophone, piano, double bass and drums (brushes). Listen to the interesting changes in rhythm and the excellent saxophone improvisations on this track.

> **CD34 I Want to Talk About You (Eckstine)**

Steel band

Groups of instruments made up from oil drums with their tops battered into shape to give them a particular pitch. Often used in carnivals and celebrations. Originated in the West Indies.

Rock bands/Pop bands

The difference between Rock, Pop and Soul bands is blurred today. Most still rely on **lead vocals** (singing the main melody) and **backing vocals** (voices accompanying the lead vocals), guitars, bass and drums. Sometimes variations are added to electric instruments and microphones to add **contrast** and make different **sections** of the music more interesting.

Here are some of the effects (FX) used:
Delay – the instant recording and reproduction of sounds, at chosen speeds.

Reverb – an effect to change the natural acoustics of a sound. 'More reverb' means that a singer using a microphone wants to sound as if they are in a larger space (a church, for example). The acoustic effect is pleasing and appears to enhance the voice.

Distortion is an effect almost exclusively used by electric guitarists. If it's good, it should be sustained, distorted and … 'dirty'!

Apart from FX, other methods of making songs more colourful can be the variation of the instruments used. Here are some variations on the guitar:
Twelve-string guitar – this gives a rich, full sound to the chords because the strings are either doubled or doubled at the octave. **Fretless bass** brings a warm and sensitive sound to a song – listen out for plenty of glissando here. (**Slapping** the bass creates yet another effect – very rhythmical and percussive and good for 'dance music'.) Even the **steel guitar** finds its way into **country** music and occasionally pop – but it is still very much associated with the Hawaiian style.

> ## What You Should Know
> - **The names and sounds of instruments in orchestras, bands and groups**
> - **The identification of these different instrumental groupings**
> - **The various techniques instrumental players employ (e.g. pizzicato)**
> - **The words used to describe special effects, instruments and how they are played**

LISTENING AND APPRAISING

GLOSSARY OF CONCEPTS

(For further detail, you should refer to a recommended music dictionary.)

a cappella – in the church style – usually unaccompanied choral music
accelerando – gradually getting faster
accent – make louder
accompany – play along with
accordion – a keyboard/button chord instrument (popular in Scottish dance bands)
acoustic – usually describing a non-electric instrument (e.g. acoustic guitar)
alberti bass – an accompanying (usually piano) bass part using the notes of a broken chord
aleatoric – a 20th-century word to describe 'chance' or 'choice' in the music's composition or performance
alto – a low female voice
anacrusis – a note (or notes) played before the first beat of the bar (the upbeat)
answer – usually a two-bar phrase answering the first two-bar phrase (the question)
arco – with the bow (usually stated on music after playing pizzicato)
aria – a song from an opera
arpeggio – a broken chord
ascending – becoming higher in pitch
atonal – where the music is not in any key (used in 20th-century music)
backing vocals – the voices in a modern group which accompany the lead vocal line
bagpipe – an instrument made up of pipes and chanter (popular in Scotland)
balafon – African xylophone-type instrument
band – any group of players (e.g. wind band, brass band, pop band, jazz band)
banjo – a stringed instrument, played like a guitar, popular in folk/country music
bar – a unit in which musical notes are placed. Divides the music rhythmically
baritone – a male voice pitched between a tenor and a bass
Baroque – a style of music in the early 17th to mid-18th century before the Classical period; applies to composers such as Bach and Handel
bass – the lowest male voice
bass guitar – has four strings; used to accompany other instruments; developed from double bass
beat – the basic unit of time used in writing and playing music
beats in the bar – system used to divide the music into organised units of time
binary music – music in two distinct parts (A and B)
blowing – the means of producing sound on instruments such as trumpet and flute
blues – an important form of early jazz, developed by Afro-Americans in the USA
blues scale – a scale (similar to a combination of major and minor) used in blues music
boogie-woogie – jazz piano style, with repetitive rhythmical bass and improvised syncopated melody
Bothy Ballad – traditional Scottish folk songs about working conditions (usually on farms)
bowing – drawing a bow across the strings
brass band – group of players using instruments such as cornet, tenor horn and euphonium
brass – name describing trombones, trumpets, french horns and tubas in the orchestra
broken chord – notes of a chord played separately e.g. C E G (like arpeggio)

cadence – 'resting point' that marks the end of phrases/sections; progression of two chords
cadenza – a flourish of notes by soloist towards end of a concerto movement
calypso – Trinidadian folk music often with words related to topical, even political issues
canon – strict form of writing where second part imitates first part (before first part ends)
cantata – an extended choral work for voices and usually orchestra (often religious)
ch'in – a Chinese plucked string instrument usually with silk strings
choral – relating to a choir or chorus
chorale – congregational hymn tune of the German church (sometimes harmonised)
chord – a combination of two or more notes played at the same time
chorus – a large body of singers who perform together
chromatic – moving in semitones; or, notes outside the major or minor key
Classical music – a style of music in latter 18th century. Simplicity of harmony, melodic and balanced; applies to composers such as Mozart and Haydn.
coda – a short section of music sometimes added at the end of a piece to 'round it off'
col legno – striking the strings (e.g. of the violin) with the wood of the bow
compound – the unit of a dotted crotchet beat divisible into thirds (e.g. $\frac{6}{8}$ $\frac{9}{8}$)
concerto – a work usually in three movements for soloist and orchestra
contrapuntal – having a musical texture in which two or more parts/voices of equal importance weave along together
contrary motion – parts or notes moving in opposite directions
contrast – used to describe changes in mood, key, speed, etc. in compositions
counter tenor – a male voice higher than tenor, similar to contralto (female)
counter melody – a second melody part which plays above the first
country – style of (mainly white) American folk music, e.g. 'bluegrass'. Original songs brought with settlers from Britain.
crescendo – gradually becoming louder
cross-rhythms – different rhythmic groupings placed against each other
dan tranh – a Vietnamese plucked string instrument
delay – an electronic effect used by guitarists and on microphones to alter the acoustic sound, e.g. to make a note or phrase repeat
descant – an additional part sung above a given melody
descending – becoming lower in pitch
diminuendo – gradually becoming softer
discord – where the notes don't 'fit' harmonically (opposite of concord)
dissonant – having discord
distortion – an effect used by guitarists to create distorted or sustained sound
dixieland – an early form of jazz, popular in the southern states of USA
djembe – an African goblet-shaped drum
double-stopping – bowing more than one string at a time (on a violin, cello, etc.) creating chords
downbeat – the first strong beat in a bar
drone – a sustained note, usually in the bass, which accompanies the melody (e.g. on bagpipes)
drum fill – a flourish of drum beats to mark the end or start of musical phrases
dundun – an African hourglass-shaped drum
electronic drums – a computer device which creates drum rhythms and patterns

GLOSSARY OF CONCEPTS

ensemble – a combination of two or more performers
episode – the music which separates the repeats of the theme in rondo form
fanfare – a flourish of trumpets; music often for state occasions, ceremonies
fiddle – a violin; called fiddle when playing in a certain style (e.g. folk music)
flutter-tonguing – method of tonguing (rolling an 'r') used by wind players to stop/start the flow of air
folk group – group playing fiddle, accordion and whistle or other 'folk' instruments
folk – style of music passed down the generations through popular songs/tunes
fretless bass – a bass guitar with no frets creating a sound similar to a double bass. Listen out for sliding notes (glissandi)
Gaelic Psalms – 'long tunes', i.e. improvised songs of worship with 'leader' and congregation, which are sung in Gaelic (usually in the Western Isles of Scotland)
Gagaku – a slow and stately Japanese music/dance form associated with the nobility
gamelan music – percussion players create melody (skeleton), using different sized 'metallophones' to decorate and develop a piece as one 'complete' sound (associated with Indonesia)
Ghanaian drum ensemble – groups/tribes from Ghana playing elaborate and exciting dance rhythms on percussion instruments, shakers and finger/ankle bells
glissando – to 'slide' through the notes in an ascending or descending 'scale'
grace notes – additional notes added to decorate a melody
ground bass – a repeated phrase or motif heard in the bass part
guitar – popular instrument with 6 (or 12) strings which are strummed or plucked
harmony – the sounding of two or more notes together
harp/clarsach – a plucked string instrument. Clarsach used in Scottish folk music
heterophony – type of music where there are several instrumental lines playing the same basic melody but each one decorates/develops the melody in their own way
homophonic – having many sounds (harmony) which move rhythmically as one, in step
hymn – religious song usually sung by congregation in church
imitation – where one theme or statement in one part is immediately imitated in another part
imperfect cadence – two chords creating 'resting point' in music, e.g. chord I to chord V; sounds unfinished
Impressionism – style of music in late 19th-century France; mood of music suggested rather than stated
improvise – make up, compose 'on the spot'
Indian music – music from India, e.g. sitar music
Indonesian gamelan ensemble – an ensemble (group) from Indonesia of gongs, 'metallophones' and drums, usually 15–20 players
inversion – notes turned upside down
inverted pedal – upper part sustained or repeated while harmonies change below
interval – the distance between two notes, e.g. C to G is a fifth; C to E is a third
jazz – a style of music which originated from Black Americans in the 19th century
jazz group – consists of instruments such as piano, bass drums, guitar, clarinet, trumpet
jig – a quick dance usually in $\frac{6}{8}$ time. Popular in Irish and Scottish folk music
kalengu – an African hourglass-shaped drum
keyboard – any instrument which uses a set of keys (e.g. piano, synthesizer, organ)
koto – a Japanese plucked string instrument

kum – a Korean plucked string instrument
Latin American music – a style of jazz dance music from South America
Latin Percussion ensemble – drums/percussion group prominent in rhythmical Latin dance music
lead vocals – singer of the main line/melody of a song; usually part of a modern band, e.g. a pop band, jazz band
leaping melody – a melody which jumps about as opposed to one which moves in steps
legato – smoothly, without breaks in the sound
major – a particular pattern of notes making up a key, chord or scale
march – a composition used for marching, usually in strict $\frac{2}{4}$ or $\frac{4}{4}$ time
melismatic – effect where lyrics or words use more than one note per syllable, e.g. plainsong
mento – Jamaican folk music including different types of song and dance
mezzo-soprano – a female voice between a soprano and alto voice
military band – a group of woodwind, brass and percussion instruments (now often described as a concert band)
minimalist – late 20th-century style where simple patterns/ostinati are developed, extended and added to each time they are repeated
minor – a particular pattern of notes which applies to key, chords and scales
minuet and trio – a musical form (ABA) popular in the Classical period
modal scale – a scale of music, not major or minor, originally used in medieval music
modulation – a change of key from that already established
mouth music (port a beul) – a kind of vocal improvisation used to accompany Scottish dance
musical – like an opera, but often more light-hearted and usually with spoken dialogue
muted – dampened, quietened (referring to the sound of an instrument)
note-cluster – 20th-century term to describe 'chord' of several adjacent notes played together
obbligato – an instrumental accompaniment part that is compulsory to the music
octave – an interval of 8 notes, having the same letter names, e.g. C – C
off the beat – where the accent is on the weak beat – as in syncopation
opera – a play that is sung and uses costumes and scenery
oratorio – music for soloists, choir and orchestra with a religious theme, in many sections
orchestra – a large group of musicians made up of woodwind, strings, brass and percussion
organ – a keyboard instrument (of various sizes), often with foot pedals and pipes
ornament – additional notes (e.g. trills or turns) added to a given passage to enhance it
ostinato – a short pattern of notes constantly repeated
pan pipes – graded sets of pipes bound together which you blow across. Often associated with Andean South America (Peru, Chile, etc.)
passing note – a note passing from one harmonic chord to the next, usually in steps
Passion – large work for orchestra, soloists and chorus, like an oratorio; including story of crucifixion of Christ
pattern – the description given to a particular rhythm or sequence of notes, e.g. an ostinato
pedal – a note sustained or repeated in the bass part while the harmonies above change
pentatonic scale – a scale made up of a pattern of five different notes
percussion – instruments which produce their sound mainly by being struck
percussive – creating effects similar to those created by percussion instruments, e.g. col legno on the violin

perfect cadence – two chords creating a 'resting point' in music, e.g. chord V to chord I. This sounds final and complete.
phrase – a group of notes expressed as one statement, as in language
pibroch – a type of Highland bagpipe music – often very elaborate
pipe band – a marching band made up of bagpipes and drums
pipes – shortened name for instruments such as bagpipes, pan pipes
pizzicato – the plucking of stringed instruments, as opposed to using the bow
plucking – pulling the strings with the fingers (pizzicato)
polyphonic – having 'many sounds', with several voices or instruments combined contrapuntally
pop – a style of modern music, usually songs, associated with 'youth culture'
pop group – a modern group who usually sing and play electric guitars and drums
programme music – music which describes a scene, a story or emotions
pulse – beat
raga – scale/mode on which Indian melodies are based
ragtime – a style of lively music (usually for piano) popular in the USA, featuring syncopation
rallentando – a direction to slow down
recitative – sung speech in opera often used to move the plot or story on
recorder – an early form of woodwind instrument, now popular in schools
reel – a dance (usually Irish or Scottish) in quick but smooth four time
register – a group of notes belonging to a particular pitch range
relative major – a major key that shares same key signature as minor key, e.g. G major and E minor; connected through modulation.
relative minor – a minor key that shares same key signature as major, e.g. D minor and F major; connected through modulation.
repetition – a passage or pattern of notes which is repeated
reverb – an effect similar to 'delay' used in amplified instruments or microphones to promote changes in acoustics, e.g. music played in a room can sound as if played in a large hall
rhythm – patterns of note values within a given pulse
riff – a short phrase, repeated frequently throughout (often used in pop and jazz)
rock – a style of modern popular music with roots in rock 'n' roll
rock group – a modern band usually with singer, electric guitars and drums
rock 'n' roll – a style of dance music popular in the 1950s, from the USA
Romantic – a style of music from the 19th century. Rich in harmony and very melodic. Includes music by composers such as Tchaikovsky and Wagner.
rondo – a composition in which the theme (A) keeps recurring (e.g. ABACADA...)
round – where the theme is started and repeated in a staggered fashion throughout parts
rubato – 'robbed time' – changes in tempo to create expression
samba – heavily syncopated Brazilian dance music, with an easy $\frac{2}{4}$ beat
salsa – rhythmical song/dance music from Cuba/Caribbean
scale – a passage of notes moving up or down in steps
scherzo – a lively movement from a symphony or sonata usually in $\frac{3}{4}$ time
Scotch snap – a short note on the beat followed by a longer one ♪♩.
Scots Ballad – a Scottish folk song, often describing a disaster; a story told through song
Scottish dance band – a band made up of fiddle, accordion, piano and drums

section – usually a particular part of a piece of music, e.g. the 'middle' section; or, a part of the orchestra, e.g. the brass section

semitone – a half tone or half step from one note to the next, e.g. F# to G

sequence – a pattern of notes usually repeated up or down one step

simple time – crotchet beats divisible into halves (e.g. $\frac{2}{4}, \frac{3}{4}, \frac{4}{4}$)

sitar – a guitar-like instrument from India with a long neck and usually 7 strings. It has a very distinctive sound.

slapping – a word used to describe a method of playing the bass guitar – to 'slap' the strings

slide guitar – stringed instrument played on a stand using a 'bottle neck' on finger. Listen out for sliding effect, e.g. as in Hawaiian music.

slow air – a simple melody in the style of a slow Scottish song, usually played on the fiddle or bagpipes

solo – a piece or passage performed by one player or singer

soprano – a high female voice

soul – a style of popular music, with black American roots, emotional; comes from gospel and blues

staccato – short detached notes

steel band – a group using oil drum tops, tuned to different pitches (from the West Indies)

stepwise – melody which moves about in steps (as opposed to jumps)

Strathspey – a traditional Scottish dance in $\frac{4}{4}$ time played at a moderate speed (features Scotch snap)

striking – hitting an instrument (normally percussion) in order to create a particular sound

strings – orchestral family of instruments including violin, viola, cello and double bass

strophic – in song, where the lyrics in each verse change but the music remains the same

strumming – a means of producing sound on instruments such as guitar and banjo

suling – Indonesian flute-like instrument

suspension – a kind of discord, where one note is held over from previous chord

sustained – where sounds are held on

swing – a popular style of dance music created in the 1930s (Big Band)

syllabic – where each syllable of a word is given a note (opposite of melismatic)

symphony – a large-scale orchestral work usually in four movements

syncopation – where the natural pulse has been shifted onto the weaker beat

tabla – a pair of Indian drums often used to accompany the sitar

tala – Indian rhythmic patterns

tama – an African hourglass-shaped drum

tenor – a high male voice

ternary – a composition in three parts: (A) first part (B) a new second part (A) first part

theme – the main melody of a piece of music

theme and variation – where the theme is stated and then altered (e.g. in speed, key, style, instruments)

through-composed – where the music changes for each stanza/verse

tierce de picardie – to end a piece of music written in a minor key with the chord of the major key of the same name. For example, a piece in key of G minor ends with the chord of G major.

tonal music – music where the key note or tonic is established (as opposed to atonal music)

transpose – to change a passage of music into a different key

transposing instruments – instruments which need to play in a different key to sound at concert pitch, e.g. Bb clarinet, french horn

tremolando/tremolo – rapid movement of the bow creating a trembling effect
trill – ornament in which two consecutive notes are played alternately and quickly
twelve-string guitar – an acoustic guitar with 12 strings, tuning as 6 string, except strings doubled or doubled at the octave
unaccompanied – with no instruments accompanying or playing along with
unison – where all parts play or sing the same notes at the same time (the opposite of harmony)
upbeat – the last beat of a bar (before the first downbeat of next bar)
vamp – improvise simple chords (usually on the piano) to accompany a tune
vibrato – an effect meaning fast fluctuations between notes; used by singers and string players to improve expression and feeling
vocal – using the voice
walking bass – a bass part which uses mainly scale passages, pinning down the beat (often used in jazz)
Waulking Song – a traditional Gaelic song performed during repetitive work
waltz – a popular dance composition in $\frac{3}{4}$ time, at a moderate pace
whole-tone – a whole-tone scale has no semitones, popular in some 20th-century music
wind/military band – band made up of woodwind, brass and percussion
woodwind – a section of the orchestra, mainly flutes, clarinets, oboes and bassoons
word painting – using music to describe words, e.g. 'here comes the rain' – instruments play short sharp sounds, increasing in volume and speed
word setting – the setting of words to music in a particular musical framework

LIST OF CD TRACKS

CD No.	Title	Composer	Performer	Recording Co.	Page
CD1	Japanese Garden	J. Montgomery	John Montgomery	Leckie & Leckie	18
CD2	Carolina Blues	J. Montgomery	John Montgomery	Leckie & Leckie	23
CD3	Jeux d'Adresse	P. Kay	John Montgomery	Leckie & Leckie	28
CD4	From a Railway Carriage	J. Montgomery	John Montgomery	Leckie & Leckie	34
CD5	Conversations	J. Montgomery	John Montgomery	Leckie & Leckie	37
CD6	Ode to Joy	Beethoven	John Montgomery	Leckie & Leckie	40
CD7	More than Words Can Say 1	J. Montgomery	vocals Brian Carty	Leckie & Leckie	47
CD8	More than Words Can Say 2	J. Montgomery	vocals Brian Carty	Leckie & Leckie	48
CD9	Bangla Dhun (from India – Ravi Shankar)	Shankar	Ravi Shankar & Ali Akbar Khan	Saar	61
CD10	Sab Vird Karo Allah Allah (World of Music Sampler)	Khan	Nusrat Fateh Ali Khan	Nascente	61
CD11	Gending Langiang (World of Drums and Percussion)	(traditional)	Sekehe Muni	CMP Records	61
CD12	Un Aeroplano A Vela (Montgolfières)	G. Testa/P. Ponzo	Gianmaria Testa (No. LBLC 2519)	Label Bleu	62
CD13	Fato Consumado (World of Music Sampler)	Djavan	Djavan	Nascente	62
CD14	La Bamba (Mexico y Salsa)	A. Gomez-Orozco	Alvara Gomez-Orozco & Band	Koka Music	62
CD15	Jump for Joy (Soca Matrix)	A. Lyons/R. Lewis	Super Blue	Rituals Music	63
CD16	Trinidad Farewell (Music of the Caribbean)	Arconte	Arconte	Phonographic Performance Ltd	63
CD17	Dance of the Woman (African Tribal Music & Dances)	(traditional)	The Malinké Tribe	Laserlight	63
CD18	Serengetti (One World)	Andy Quin	Ethno Technic	Global	64
CD19	Rokudan (Koto Music of Japan)	(traditional)	Zumi-Kai	Laserlight	64
CD20	Sweet Talkin' Rag	J. Montgomery	John Montgomery	Leckie & Leckie	66

CD No.	Title	Composer	Performer	Recording Co.	Page
CD21	The Hallelujah Chorus (from The Messiah)	Handel	Acad. & Chorus St Martin's (No. 444 824-2, P7925)	Decca	71
CD22	O Mio Babbino Caro (from Gianni Schicchi)	Puccini	Lesley Garrett/ Philharmonia Orch. (No. PCD 2709)	Telstar Records	72
CD23	Beautiful As You	A. Montgomery	John Montgomery	Leckie & Leckie	73
CD24	Prélude à l'après-midi d'un faune	Debussy	London Symphony Orchestra (No. 455152-2)	Decca	75
CD25	The Rite of Spring	Stravinsky	L'Orchestre de la Suisse Romande (No. 443467-2)	Decca	76
CD26	Classical Symphony No. 1 Gavotta	Prokofiev	Orpheus Chamber Orchestra (No. 423 624-2)	Deutsche Grammophon	76
CD27	Music for Strings, Percussion and Celeste	Bartók	Boston Symphony Orchestra (No. 439 402-2)	Deutsche Grammophon	76
CD28	Fugue No. 16 in G Minor (from 48 Preludes & Fugues)	Bach	John Montgomery	Leckie & Leckie	78
CD29	Horn Concerto No. 4 (3rd Movement)	Mozart	Peter Damm/ASMIF (No. 426 207-2 Vol 2)	Philips Classic Productions	79
CD30	Violin Concerto in D Major (1st Movement)	Brahms	Joshua Bell/ Cleveland Symphony Orchestra (No. 444 811-2 PY925)	Decca	80
CD31	Mars (from The Planets Suite)	Holst	London Symphony Orchestra	ABM Music	80
CD32	A Life on the Ocean Wave	Russell	Royal Marines	Grasmere Records	82
CD33	Tritsch-Tratsch Polka	Strauss	Williams-Pairey Engin. Band (No. STCD242)	Grasmere Records	82
CD34	I Want to Talk About You	Eckstine	John Coltrane (No. ST9647, STCD 248)	Charly Schallplatten	82

Leckie & Leckie's GCSE Music CD ℗ 2001 Leckie & Leckie. All rights of the producer and of the owner of the works reproduced reserved. Unauthorised copying, hiring, lending, public performance and broadcasting of this CD is prohibited. MCPS.